audepublishing.com

First Hardcover Edition 2021.

Hardcover ISBN 9780578306049

Paperback ISBN 9798486794483

eISBN 9780578305547

To request permissions, contact jon@audepublishing.com

Bitcoin: Answered

A Beginner's Guide to Everything Bitcoin

Jon Law & Alan John

Table of Contents

Bitcoin: Answered 2

    A Beginner's Guide to Everything Bitcoin.......................... 2

Bitcoin: Answered 8

    What is Bitcoin?... 11

    Who started Bitcoin?.. 12

    How does Bitcoin work? 13

    What is the history of Bitcoin? 15

    What are Bitcoin addresses?... 17

    What is a Bitcoin node? 18

    What kind of Bitcoin wallets are there?......................... 19

    Is Bitcoin mining profitable?... 21

    Are there real, physical Bitcoins?.................................. 25

    Is Bitcoin frictionless?.. 26

    Does Bitcoin use mnemonic phrases?............................ 27

    Can you get Bitcoin back if you send it to the wrong address?28

    Is Bitcoin secure? 29

    Will Bitcoin run out?.. 31

    What is the point of Bitcoin?... 32

    How would you explain Bitcoin to a 5-year-old? 33

    Is Bitcoin a company? 34

    Is Bitcoin a scam?... 35

    Can Bitcoin be hacked?.. 36

    Who keeps track of Bitcoin transactions?...................... 37

    Can anyone buy and sell Bitcoin?................................. 38

    Is Bitcoin anonymous?... 39

Can the rules of Bitcoin change?..40

Should the word Bitcoin be capitalized?..................................41

What are Bitcoin protocols? 42

What is Bitcoin's ledger?..43

What kind of network is Bitcoin? 44

Can Bitcoin still be the top cryptocurrency when it reaches its

max supply?..45

How much money do Bitcoin miners make?...........................46

What is the block height of Bitcoin?...47

Does Bitcoin use atomic swaps? 48

What are Bitcoin mining pools?...49

Who are the largest Bitcoin miners?...50

Is Bitcoin technology outdated?..51

Are there multiple types of nodes?...53

How does the supply mechanism of Bitcoin work?...............54

How is the market cap of Bitcoin calculated? 55

Can you give and get Bitcoin loans? 56

What are the largest problems with Bitcoin?...........................57

Does Bitcoin have coins or tokens? 59

Can you earn money just by holding Bitcoin?.........................61

Does Bitcoin have slippage? 62

What Bitcoin acronyms should I know?...................................63

What Bitcoin slang should I know? 66

Can you use leverage or margin to trade Bitcoin? 70

Who owns Bitcoin? 74

How do you read a Bitcoin chart? 75

    Charting Resources 85

What is a Bitcoin bubble?...88

5

What does "bullish" and "bearish" mean for Bitcoin?.................. 89

Is Bitcoin cyclical?.. 90

What is Bitcoin's utility? 91

Is it better to hold Bitcoin or trade it? 92

Is investing in Bitcoin risky? 93

What is the Bitcoin white paper?... 94

What are Bitcoin keys? 96

Is Bitcoin scarce?.. 97

What are Bitcoin whales? 98

Who are Bitcoin miners? 99

What does it mean to "burn" Bitcoin?................................ 100

What does it mean that Bitcoin is inflationary? 101

What is Bitcoin's volume? 103

How is Bitcoin mined? 104

Can you get USD with Bitcoin? 105

What is a Bitcoin pair?... 106

Is Bitcoin better than Ethereum?...................................... 107

Can you buy things with Bitcoin?...................................... 108

How do you buy Bitcoin?.. 110

Is Bitcoin a good investment?... 111

Will Bitcoin crash?.. 112

What is Bitcoin's PoW system?... 113

What is Bitcoin halving?... 114

Why is Bitcoin volatile? 116

Should I invest in Bitcoin?.. 117

How do I successfully invest in Bitcoin? 118

Does Bitcoin have intrinsic value?..................................... 124

Does Bitcoin get taxed? 125

Does Bitcoin trade 24/7?..127

Does Bitcoin use fossil fuels?...128

Will Bitcoin hit 100k?...129

Will Bitcoin hit 1 million?..130

Will Bitcoin keep going up this fast?...............................131

What are Bitcoin forks?..132

Why does Bitcoin fluctuate?..133

How do Bitcoin wallets work?...134

Does Bitcoin work in all countries?.................................135

How many people have Bitcoin?..137

Who has the most Bitcoin?...138

Can you trade Bitcoin with algorithms?..........................139

How will Bitcoin affect the future?..................................146

Is Bitcoin the future of money?..148

How many people are Bitcoin billionaires?....................150

Are there secret Bitcoin billionaires?..............................152

Will Bitcoin reach mainstream adoption?.......................153

Will Bitcoin get taken over by other cryptocurrencies?..........154

Can Bitcoin change from PoW?...155

Was Bitcoin the first ever cryptocurrency?....................156

Can Bitcoin be more than an alternative to gold?.....................158

What is the latency of Bitcoin, and is it important?.................159

What are some Bitcoin conspiracy theories?...................160

Why do most other coins often follow Bitcoin?.............161

What is Bitcoin Cash?...162

How will Bitcoin act during a recession?........................163

Can Bitcoin survive in the long run?...............................164

What is the end goal of Bitcoin and cryptos?................165

Is Bitcoin too expensive to use as a cryptocurrency? 166

How popular is Bitcoin? 168

Resources 169

Crypto Essential Dictionary 171

Books 190

Exchanges 191

Podcasts 192

News Services 193

Charting Services 194

YouTube Channels 195

References 197

Endnotes 204

Bitcoin: Answered

Bitcoin: Answered is an attempt at disentangling the fragmented web of information around Bitcoin being received by the general public. Regardless of personal attitudes toward cryptocurrencies and Bitcoin (most of which, for those not studied, are either overly optimistic or overly cynical), the reach of cryptocurrency is growing at such a rate and being installed in the financial ecosystem at such a rate, that not understanding the baseline history, concepts, and feasibility of Bitcoin is much more damaging than not. You will hopefully find this information quite fascinating; Bitcoin was the first of an entirely new way of thinking about money and transacting value. By the end, you will understand the scope of Bitcoin, digital currencies, and blockchain; many of these systems, as should be noted, are comparable only in the loosest of senses, and the potential and applicable use cases of such technology are quite astounding, especially given that the ecosystem of fiat currency has changed little since the removal of currencies from the gold standard a half-century ago. In such a sense, to think of all cryptocurrencies as Bitcoin and of Bitcoin as a fringe bubble is simply wrong; yes, Bitcoin is far from perfect, but there is so much more to what is, essentially, the digitalization and decentralization of value. This book tackles all these concepts and more through a simple, question-based format, starting with "What is Bitcoin?" You may skim the book as per your knowledge or read cover-to-cover; either way, my hope and the hope of my team is that you leave this book with an understanding of Bitcoin from a sentimental, technical, historical, and conceptual standpoint, as well as alongside a continued interest and desire to learn more. Further resources can be found at the back of the book.

Now, onward we traverse, in the noble pursuit of knowledge.

Enjoy the book.

What is Bitcoin?

Bitcoin is many things: an open-source, peer-to-peer computer network, a collection of protocols, a digital gold, and a cryptocurrency. In the physical, Bitcoin is 13,000 computers running various protocols and algorithms. In concept, Bitcoin is a global means of easy and secure transaction, a democratizing force, and a means of both transparent and anonymous finance. In the bridge between physical and conceptual, Bitcoin is a cryptocurrency; a means and store of value that exists purely online, without any physical form. All this, however, is like asking the question, "What is money?" and responding, "pieces of paper." One not familiar with Bitcoin who reads the above paragraph will almost certainly come away with more questions than answers; for this reason, the question, "What is Bitcoin?" is, in essence, the question of this book, and through an analysis of each part, you may hopefully arrive at an understanding of the whole.

Who started Bitcoin?

Satoshi Nakamoto is the individual, or possibly the group of individuals, who created Bitcoin. Not much is known about this mysterious figure, and his anonymity has spawned countless theories. While Nakamoto listed himself as a 45-year-old male from Japan on an official peer-to-peer foundations website, he uses British idioms in his emails. Additionally, the timestamps of his work align better with someone based in the US or the UK. Regardless of his identity, what remains a fact is that the creator of Bitcoin currently holds a fortune worth more than $50 billion (equivalent to 1.1 million bitcoins) and if Bitcoin goes up another few hundred percent, the father of cryptocurrency will become the richest individual in the world.

How does Bitcoin work?

Bitcoin and all cryptocurrencies operate through Blockchain technology. Blockchain, in its most basic form, can be thought of as a type of network that stores data in literal chains of blocks. Here is exactly how blocks and chains come into play:

- Each "block" stores digital information, such as the time, date, amount, etc. of transactions.

- The block stores the identity of participants in a transaction by using "digital keys," which are strings of numbers and letters that are received when opening a wallet. Wallets hold crypto assets.

- However, blocks cannot operate on their own. Blocks need verification from other computers, aka "nodes" in the network.

- The other nodes will validate the information of one block. Once they validate the data, and if everything looks good, the block and the associated will be stored on the public ledger.

- The public ledger is a database that records every single approved transaction ever made on the network. Most cryptocurrencies, including Bitcoin, have their own public ledger.

- Each block in the ledger is linked to the block that came before it and the block that came after it. Hence, the links the blocks form create a chain-like pattern, and a blockchain is formed.

Summary: The **block** represents digital information, and the **chain** represents how that data is stored in the database.

So, to recap our earlier definition, blockchain is a new type of database, and Bitcoin's blockchain allows users to transact the coin. Blockchains are an important concept, so don't worry if you haven't got it down yet. Plenty more on the subject is coming.

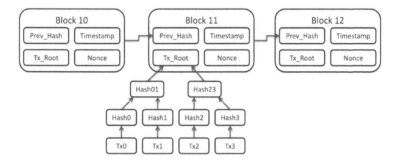

[i] Above is a visualized breakdown of each block in the network.

15

What is the history of Bitcoin?

This is a brief history of cryptocurrency, blockchain, and Bitcoin. An in-depth prehistory of Bitcoin is further along in the book (under the question, "Was Bitcoin the first cryptocurrency?").

In 1991, a cryptographically secured chain of blocks was conceptualized for the first time. Nearly a decade later, in 2000, Stegan Knost published a theory on cryptography secured chains, as well as ideas for practical implementation. In 2008, Satoshi Nakamoto released a white paper (a white paper being a thorough report and guide) establishing a model for a blockchain and in 2009 Nakamoto implemented the first blockchain, which he used to create Bitcoin. Since launch, Bitcoin has grown into a trillion-dollar asset while also furthering the successful applications of blockchain technologies and decentralized applications.

Bitcoin Price History

How many Bitcoins are there?

Bitcoin has a maximum supply of 21 million coins. As of 2021, there are 18.7 million bitcoins in circulation, meaning just 2.3 million remain out of circulation. Of that number, 900 new Bitcoin are added to the circulating supply each day through mining rewards.[1] Mining rewards are the rewards given to computers that solve complex equations to process and verify Bitcoin transactions. The people who run these computers are called "miners." Anyone can start Bitcoin mining; even a basic PC can become a node (remember, a node is a computer in the network) and start mining.

MAXIMUM SUPPLY: 21 MILLION

CIRCULATING SUPPLY: 18 MILLION

What are Bitcoin addresses?

An address, also known as a public key, is a unique collection of numbers and letters that function as an identification code, comparable to a bank account number or an email address. With it, you can carry out transactions on the blockchain. Addresses connect to a base blockchain; for example, a Bitcoin address lies on the Bitcoin blockchain. Each time you send or receive cryptocurrency, you will use an associated address. Addresses, however, cannot store assets; they merely serve as identifiers that point towards wallets, in which the assets are actually stored. Private keys, on the other hand, pair with your public key (your public address) and allow you to access your holdings.

Bitcoin Address

SHARE

1DpQP4yKSGWXWrXNkm1YNYBTqEweuQcyYg

Private Key

SECRET

L4NhQX1DFJpFAJJYAHKkpukerqxtjF1XhvR5J2PQcnDparA2vD9M [2]

Bitcoin address example: 1BvBESEystWetqTFn3Au6u4FGg7xJaAQN5

What is a Bitcoin node?

A node is a computer connected to a blockchain's network that assists the blockchain in writing and validating blocks, as well as in receiving and sending information. Collectively, the entire distributed nature of Bitcoin and cryptocurrencies, as well as many of the underlying blockchain and security features, are enabled by the concept and utilization of a global, node-based system.

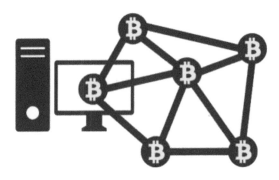

What kind of Bitcoin wallets are there?

Several distinct categories of wallets exist and differ in security, usability, and accessibility:

Paper Wallets. A paper wallet defines the storage of private information (public keys, private keys, and seed phrases) on paper. This works because any public and private key pair can form a wallet; no online interface is needed. To create a Bitcoin paper wallet, anyone can visit bitaddress.org to generate a public address and a private key, and then print the information. The QR codes and key strings can be used to facilitate transactions. Given the challenges facing paper wallet holders (water damage, accidental loss, obscurity) relative to ultra-secure online options, paper wallets are no longer recommended for use in managing significant holdings.

Hot Wallets/Cold Wallets. A hot wallet refers to a wallet that is connected to the internet; the opposite, cold storage, refers to a wallet that is not connected to the internet. Hot wallets allow for the owner of the account to send and receive tokens; while cold storage is more secure than hot storage and offers many of the benefits of paper wallets without as much risk. Most exchanges allow users to move holdings from hot wallets (which is the default) to cold wallets with the press of a few buttons (Coinbase refers to cold/offline storage as a "vault"). To withdraw holdings from cold storage requires a few days, which circles back to the accessibility versus security dynamic between hot storage and cold storage. If you're interested in holding a crypto asset for the long-term, cold storage within your exchange is the way to go. If you plan to actively trade or engage in the trading of holdings, cold storage is not a feasible option.

Hardware Wallets. Hardware wallets are physical devices that store your private key. This option allows for some degree of online accessibility (since hardware wallets render it very easy to access holdings) to be combined with a means of storage that isn't connected to the internet and is, therefore, more secure. Some popular hardware wallets, such as Ledger even offer apps that work in unison with hardware wallets without compromising security. Overall, hardware wallets are a great option for serious and long-term holders, although physical security must be accounted for; such wallets, as well as paper wallets, are best stored in banks or high-end storage solutions.

Is Bitcoin mining profitable?

It certainly can be. The average annual return on investment for those who rent the computational power (the rigs and nodes) of other miners can vary from high-single digits to low double-digits, while the annual ROI for self-managed Bitcoin mining varies throughout the double-digits (to put a number on it, 40% to 200% annually can be expected, while 50% to 150% is normal). Either way, this return beats the historical stock market and real estate returns of 10%. However, Bitcoin mining is volatile and expensive, and a swath of factors influence each individual's returns. In the next question, we'll examine factors of Bitcoin mining profitability, which provides much better insight into estimated returns, as well as insight into why some time periods and miners perform exceptionally well, while some don't.

What influences Bitcoin mining profitability?

The following variables are essential to determining the potential profitability of Bitcoin mining:

Cryptocurrency Price. The major influencing factor in mining profit is the price of the given cryptocurrency asset. A 2x rise in Bitcoin price results in 2x the mining profit (because the amount of Bitcoin being earned stays the same, while the equivalent value changes), while a 50% drop results in half the profits. Most miners must sell earnings to cover costs, which renders price action (especially given the volatile nature of cryptocurrencies and especially that of Bitcoin) extremely important. If a miner can afford not to sell and holds for the long-term, then price becomes less important.

Hash Rate and Difficulty. Hash Rate is the speed at which equations are solved and blocks are found. Hash rate for miners roughly equates to earnings, and more miners entering the system (thus increasing the hash rate of the network and the related mining difficulty, which is a term that describes how hard it is to mine blocks) dilutes per-miner hash share and therefore profitability. In this way, competition drives profit down through difficulty and hash rate.

Price of Electricity. As the mining process becomes more difficult, electricity requirements also increase. The price of electricity can become a major player in profitability.

Halving. Every 4 years, the block rewards programmed into Bitcoin halve to incrementally reduce the influx of coins. Currently (since May 13th, 2020, and lasting until 2024), miner rewards are 6.25 bitcoin per block. However, in 2024, block rewards will fall to 3.125 bitcoin per block, and so on. In this manner, long-term mining rewards must fall unless the value of each coin rises as much or more than the equivalent decrease in block rewards.

Hardware Cost. Of course, the actual price of the hardware needed to mine Bitcoin plays an extremely large part in profit and ROI. Mining can be set up easily on normal PCs (if you have one, check out nicehash.com); that said, setting up full rigs involves the cost of motherboards, CPUs, graphics cards, GPUs, RAM, ASICs, and more. The easy way out is simply to buy pre-made rigs, but this involves paying a premium. Making your own saves money, but also requires technical knowledge. Generally, do-it-yourself options cost at least a few thousand dollars.

To conclude this question, the variables influencing mining profitability are numerous and subject to rapid change, and potential earnings are biased towards large farms with access to cheap electricity. That said, crypto mining is certainly still very much profitable, and returns (excluding the potential of a market-wide collapse) have been and likely will, for quite a while, remain far ahead of expected stock market returns or of normal returns in most other asset classes.

Are there real, physical Bitcoins?

There are not and likely will never be physical Bitcoin since it was envisioned purely as a digital currency. That said, the accessibility of Bitcoin will increase over time through better exchanges, Bitcoin ATMs, Bitcoin debit and credit cards, and other services. Hopefully, cryptocurrencies will eventually be as easy to use as physical currencies and thus nullify any physical advantages fiat currencies have over Bitcoin.

Is Bitcoin frictionless?

A frictionless market is an ideal trading environment in which no costs or restraints exist on transactions, and "frictionless" generally refers to a lack of obstacles throughout a given process. The market of Bitcoin (in regard to the transactional ecosystem), while on the road to frictionless (especially regarding global money transfer), is not close to truly being there. This is mostly the fault of adoption since Bitcoin is not currently a generally accepted unit of account nor means of payment. So, the limiting factor of Bitcoin's friction in the global transactional ecosystem isn't a fault of Bitcoin itself, but rather of the environment around Bitcoin. Even within the ecosystem of Bitcoin, fees and slow transaction speeds will likely impede Bitcoin from ever reaching a frictionless state or anywhere near that. Other cryptocurrencies are superior is this regard.

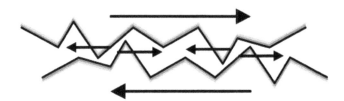

Does Bitcoin use mnemonic phrases?

A mnemonic phrase is an equivalent term to a seed phrase; both represent 12-to-24-word sequences that identify and represent wallets. Think of it as a backup password; with it, you can never lose access to your account. On the flip side, if you forget it, there's no way to reset it or get it back, and anyone with it has complete access to your wallet. All wallets within which Bitcoins are held use mnemonic phrases. You should always keep these phrases in a secure and private location; on paper or in an online password-managing service is best, best of all on paper in a safe or bank.

Your Seed Phrase

Your Seed Phrase is used to generate and recover your account.

1. issue	2. flame	3. sample
4. lyrics	5. find	6. vault
7. announce	8. banner	9. cute
10. damage	11. civil	12. goat

Please save these 12 words on a piece of paper. The order is important. This seed will allow you to recover your account.

iii

Can you get Bitcoin back if you send it to the wrong address?

A refund address is a wallet address that can serve as a backup in case a transaction fails. If such an event occurs, then a chargeback is given to the specified refund address. If you ever need to provide a refund address, make sure that the address is correct and can receive the token you're sending. That said, if a transaction goes through and registers as sent, it is impossible to get it back without the receiving party sending it back via a second transaction.

15kHAjwmMcFGsviYWrdZvvXj67gAvZJ6au

Is Bitcoin secure?

Bitcoin, governed by an underlying blockchain network, is one of the most secure systems in the world for the following reasons:

Bitcoin is public. Bitcoin, like many cryptocurrencies, has a public ledger that records all transactions. Since no private information must be provided to own and trade Bitcoin and all transaction information is public on the blockchain, intruders have nothing to hack into or steal; the only alternative to hacking into and profiting off the Bitcoin network (excluding human points of failure, such as in exchange attacks and lost passwords; we're focusing on Bitcoin itself) is a 51% attack, which, at the scale of Bitcoin, is practically impossible. Being "public" also ties into Bitcoin being permissionless; no one controls it, and therefore no subjective or singular viewpoint can affect the entire network (without the consent of everyone else in the network).

Bitcoin is decentralized. Bitcoin currently operates through 12,000+ nodes, all of which collectively serve to validate transactions.[iv] Since the entire network validates transactions, there's no way of altering or controlling transactions unless, again, 51% of the network is controlled. Such an attack, as mentioned, is practically impossible; at the current price of Bitcoin, an attacker would need to spend tens of millions of dollars a day and control a volume of computational resources that simply isn't available.[v] Hence, the decentralized nature of data validation makes Bitcoin extremely secure.

Bitcoin is irreversible. Once transactions in the network are confirmed, the change is permanent since each block (each block being a batch of new transactions) is connected to blocks on either side of it, hence forming an interconnected chain. Once written, blocks cannot be modified. These two factors, in combination, prevent data alteration, and ensure greater security.

Bitcoin uses the hashing process. A hash is a function that converts one value into another; a hash in the crypto world converts an input of letters and numbers (a string) into an encrypted output of a fixed size. Hashes help with encryption because "solving" each hash requires working backwards to solve an extremely complex mathematical problem. Hence, the ability to solve these equations is purely based on computational power. Hashing has the following benefits: data is compressed, hash values can be compared (as opposed to comparing data in its original form), and hashing functions are notably one of the most secure and breach-proof means of data transmission at large scale

Will Bitcoin run out?

It depends on what you mean by "run out." The amount of bitcoin added to the network each year will, invariably, run out. At such a point, all 21 million coins will be owned and exist within the network. However, when this happens around the year 2140, different supply mechanisms (as opposed to bitcoins being the mining reward) will take over and business will go on as normal.

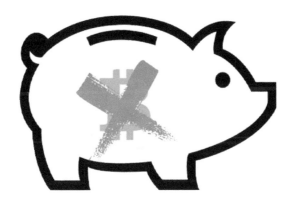

What is the point of Bitcoin?

The primary value of Bitcoin comes from its applications as a store of value and a means of private, global, and secure transactions. This, in essence, is the point of Bitcoin; a purpose which had been executed upon quite successfully, given its historical returns and the 300,000 or so daily transactions.

How would you explain Bitcoin to a 5-year-old?

Bitcoin is computer money that people can use to buy and sell things or to make more money. Bitcoin works because of blockchain. Blockchain is a tool that allows many different people to safely pass around valuable information or money without needing someone else to do it for them. People store their information and money in online wallets and use numbers and letters to find each other's wallets.

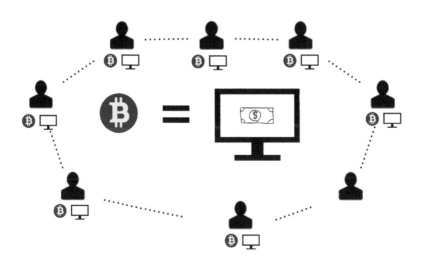

Is Bitcoin a company?

Bitcoin is not a company. It is a network of computers running algorithms. However, given the progression of software and hardware over time and to prevent the antiquation of Bitcoin, a voting system was implemented in the network at creation to allow for updates to the code and algorithms. The voting system is completely open-source and consensus-based, meaning that updates to the system proposed by developers and volunteers must undergo rigorous scrutiny from other interested parties (since an error in an update hurts all investors), and the update will only pass if mass consensus is reached. Additionally, the Bitcoin Foundation employs several full-time developers who work to establish a roadmap for Bitcoin and develop updates. Again, however, anyone with something to contribute may do so, and no actual company or organization has any degree of control over Bitcoin. Additionally, users are not forced to update if a rule change is applied; they may stick with any version they want. The ideas behind this system are quite unprecedented, and the concept of an independent, open-sourced, consensus-based network has applications across many more fields than just that of Bitcoin and cryptocurrencies.

Is Bitcoin a scam?

Bitcoin, by definition, is not a scam. It is a financial instrument created by a team of established engineers. It's worth trillions, practically impossible to hack, and the founder has yet to sell holdings.[3] That said, Bitcoin is certainly manipulatable and highly volatile. Many other cryptocurrencies on the market, unlike Bitcoin, are a scam. So, do your research, invest in established coins with reputable teams, and use common sense while making investment decisions.

Can Bitcoin be hacked?

Bitcoin itself is impossible to hack since the entire network is constantly being reviewed by many nodes (computers) within the network, and therefore any attacker can only truly hack the system if they control 51% or more of the computational power in the network (since majority control can be used to validate anything, whether it's correct or not). Given the mining power behind Bitcoin, this is essentially impossible. However, the weak point in cryptocurrency security are the wallets of users; wallets and exchanges are much easier to hack. So, although Bitcoin is impossible to hack, your Bitcoin may be hacked by the fault of an exchange or by a weak or accidently shared password. Generally, if you stick with established exchanges and keep a private, secure password, your chances of getting hacked are practically nil.

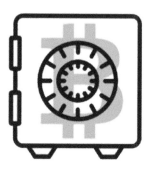 

Who keeps track of Bitcoin transactions?

Each node (computer) in the Bitcoin network maintains a complete copy of all Bitcoin transactions. Such information is used to validate transactions and ensure security. All Bitcoin transactions are public and viewable through the Bitcoin ledger; you may view the ledger for yourself at the following link:

blockchain.com/btc/unconfirmed-transactions

Can anyone buy and sell Bitcoin?

Since Bitcoin is decentralized, anyone can buy and sell, regardless of external factors or identity. That said, many countries require cryptocurrencies to be traded only through centralized exchanges (for tax and security purposes), hence requiring basic KYC mandates, such as identity, SSN, etc. Such laws do prevent some people from investing in crypto and centralized exchanges reserve the right to shut down accounts for any reason.

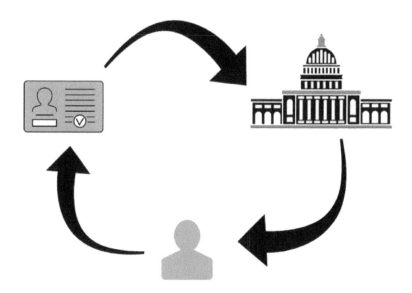

Is Bitcoin anonymous?

As mentioned in the question directly above, the innate system that governs Bitcoin allows for complete personal anonymity; all that must be shared for a successful transaction is a wallet address. However, government mandates have made it illegal in many countries (the primary example being the US) to trade on exchanges that allow for complete anonymity. Hence, centralized exchanges bar such legal anonymity while trading crypto.

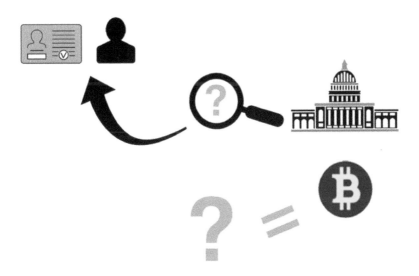

Can the rules of Bitcoin change?

Since Bitcoin is decentralized, the system cannot change itself. However, the rules of the network can be changed through the consensus of Bitcoin holders. Today, open-source projects update Bitcoin if updates are needed and do so only if the changes are accepted by the Bitcoin community.

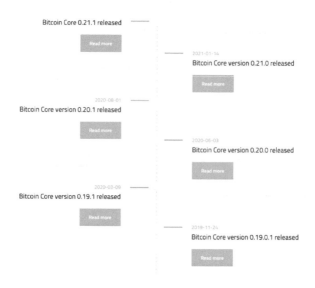

Bitcoin core updates from *bitcoin.org*.

Should the word Bitcoin be capitalized?

Bitcoin as a network should be capitalized. Bitcoin as a unit should not be capitalized. For example, "After I heard about the idea of Bitcoin, I bought 10 bitcoins."

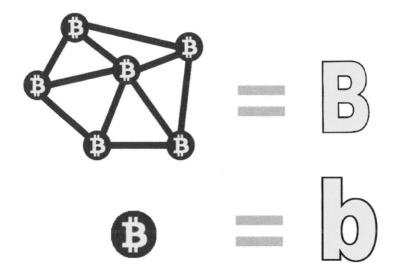

What are Bitcoin protocols?

A protocol is a system or procedure that controls how something should be done. Within cryptocurrency and Bitcoin, protocols are the governing layer of code. For example, a security protocol determines how security should be carried out, a blockchain protocol governs how blockchain acts and operates, and a Bitcoin protocol controls how Bitcoin functions.

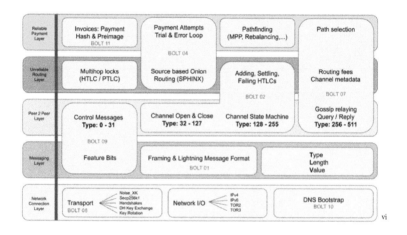

This is an example of a protocol, viewed through the lens of the Lightning Network, which is a layer-2 payment protocol designed to work on top of coins such as Bitcoin and Litecoin to enable faster transactions and thus solve scalability issues.

What is Bitcoin's ledger?

All blockchain ledgers (including that of Bitcoin) store data about financial transactions made on a given blockchain. Cryptocurrencies use public ledgers, which means the ledger is publicly available. You can see the public ledger of Bitcoin at blockchain.com/explorer.

Hash	Time	Amount (BTC)	Amount (USD)
e3bc0fb2e5f235094f3825ab722ca4dda006c3526db1466012e1395984f8a3ec	12:22	3.40547680 BTC	$170,416.94
80c2a1a69cc9fc94f082w707640218f3898beb189428840adf169fb2fb150735	12:22	0.52284473 BTC	$26,164.21
f3772b98dd9b10777e0761dd7d8be8e7953b190546b245fcafef5494124a0e9d	12:22	0.03063826 BTC	$1,533.20
e5e5e9678e6494bb68cea67eef3aee789ef972172db5424797dcd16eb7345a9a	12:22	0.00151322 BTC	$75.72
5f3bcd4212f05ed0d9ad7be40a97e1b4e6fe3456c7d9926e8b1a5219b7a1f33e	12:22	0.84369401 BTC	$42,220.15
37e7a56509c2b095549c3f865e2dcd3c0a29f47d5987d64ef5cf4b8ce9992611	12:22	0.00153592 BTC	$76.86
ee7a933c2da6c25125a653903828db74303d2efafdf730b0cc2767d8840e1754	12:22	0.00210841 BTC	$105.51
d2259896d076a2723259cc55e7131c3d4622ce6a14c37eb51cadd9992f3873c1	12:22	0.00251375 BTC	$125.79
8f7a795196ec4bdb0cc9316e75c13ca1f944c7946faf24004952aa2a0aed072f	12:22	1.60242873 BTC	$80,188.77
7f6fa2f64999a07e03a344aed9ddb34282683afeddfcb61f996109b83bdb11f	12:22	0.00022207 BTC	$11.11
8c9dfdf9b649a1d465d5d2cfcb3185ad91b067d36b4b60b3233d0c78cf859d60	12:22	0.00006000 BTC	$3.00
4dce5a8630641314fff08a30dca8209585563c450accdf01f1f72401b9ffbe24	12:22	0.00761070 BTC	$380.85
7e31b8588d549a894819ed19b11d03025141ca429bfbaf699ca73fb82ea0825d	12:22	0.00070666 BTC	$35.36
9fd5d4a37f766c414078c8d2dc8cd48efa6cf00f901d81e81e73a1a874c2beef	12:22	0.00061789 BTC	$30.92
b4dda5555fde5282c1e51fa69e56998e55904b77da989136a62b25Baac2960fb	12:22	0.07876440 BTC	$3,941.53
a8f05bce5ca3964bd5fbfb65a52e8a718345977391182Bc36Bfbc8aba128391a	12:22	1.41705545 BTC	$70,912.32
b80588be59e4be8d3b22294d86c2f0df577a7e58a92961afbb62ba3add06b053	12:22	0.30358853 BTC	$15,192.18
e0fb0dcd87c22b2e11af7eb3852a7a6a51bca0907d0d63199f6d9e275a410dd8	12:22	0.00712366 BTC	$356.48
f60389c978d4bf66bb32047fbd5efecb046d1f0e09c3c7b2035e5b2b6a852445	12:22	0.00029789 BTC	$14.91
a820e18a7a4538e4cd410f1f9fb213408174f699ffe2d245540b388e7befbfbf	12:22	0.79690506 BTC	$39,878.74
cbdc6ef0669d4a243add5c0b8c40d014d4a33a5e01e8eacd3fbcaffc9aba36c2	12:22	0.54677419 BTC	$27,361.68

*Live view of the Bitcoin public ledger from blockchain.com

What kind of network is Bitcoin?

Bitcoin is a P2P (peer-to-peer) network. A peer-to-peer network involves many computers working with each other to complete tasks. Peer-to-peer networks do not require a central authority and are an integral part of blockchain networks and cryptocurrencies.

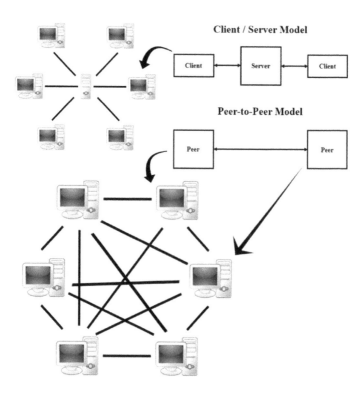

Can Bitcoin still be the top cryptocurrency when it reaches its max supply?

The supply of Bitcoin will indeed run out, but it will do so in the year 2140. At that point, all 21 million BTC will be in the network, and another incentive or supply system must be implemented for the continued survival of the network. However, guessing whether Bitcoin will be the top cryptocurrency in the year 2140 is like asking in the year 1900 what 2020 would be like; the difference in technology is almost impossibly large and the technological environment in the 22nd century is anyone's guess.

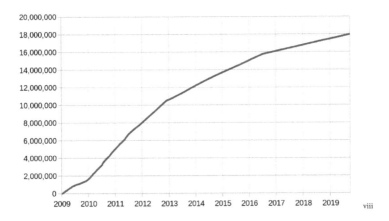

*Number of bitcoins in circulation.

How much money do Bitcoin miners make?

Bitcoin miners collectively make around $45 million per day, which equates to $1.9 million an hour and $30,000 a minute (6.25 bitcoin per block, 144 blocks per day). Per-miner profit depends on hashing power, electricity cost, pool fee (if in a pool), power consumption, and hardware cost; online mining calculators can estimate profits based on all these factors. The most popular of these calculators, provided by Nicehash, can be found at nicehash.com/profitability-calculator. The visual below displays the per-day profitability of popular mining machines as of 2019.

Model	Release	Hashrate	Power	Noise	Algo	Profitability
Bitmain Antminer S17+ (73Th)	Dec 2019	73 Th/s	2920 w	75 db	SHA-256	$9.18 /day
ASICminer 8 Nano Pro	May 2018	76 Th/s	4000 w	48 db	SHA-256	$8.40 /day
MicroBT Whatsminer M20S	Aug 2019	68 Th/s	3360 w	75 db	SHA-256	$7.78 /day
Bitmain Antminer S17e (64Th)	Nov 2019	64 Th/s	2880 w	80 db	SHA-256	$7.66 /day
Bitmain Antminer T17+ (64Th)	Dec 2019	64 Th/s	3200 w	75 db	SHA-256	$7.28 /day
StrongU STU-U8 Pro	Sep 2019	60 Th/s	2800 w	76 db	SHA-256	$7.06 /day
Bitmain Antminer S17 (56Th)	Apr 2019	56 Th/s	2520 w	82 db	SHA-256	$6.71 /day
Bitmain Antminer S17 Pro (53Th)	Apr 2019	53 Th/s	2094 w	82 db	SHA-256	$6.70 /day
Innosilicon T3+ 52T	May 2019	52 Th/s	2800 w	75 db	SHA-256	$6.39 /day
Bitmain Antminer S17 (53Th)	Apr 2019	53 Th/s	2385 w	82 db	SHA-256	$6.35 /day
Bitfury Tardis	Nov 2018	80 Th/s	6300 w	80 db	SHA-256	$6.34 /day
Bitmain Antminer S17 Pro (50Th)	Apr 2019	50 Th/s	1975 w	82 db	SHA-256	$6.32 /day

What is the block height of Bitcoin?

The block height is the number of blocks in a blockchain. Height 0 is the first block (also referred to as the "genesis block"), height 1 is the second block, and so on; the current block height of Bitcoin is more than half a million. The "block generation time" of Bitcoin is currently around 10 minutes, meaning one new block is added to the Bitcoin blockchain approximately every 10 minutes.

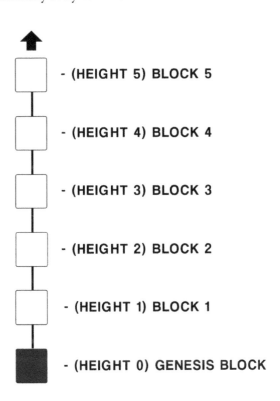

- (HEIGHT 5) BLOCK 5

- (HEIGHT 4) BLOCK 4

- (HEIGHT 3) BLOCK 3

- (HEIGHT 2) BLOCK 2

- (HEIGHT 1) BLOCK 1

- (HEIGHT 0) GENESIS BLOCK

Does Bitcoin use atomic swaps?

An atomic swap is a smart contract technology that allows users to exchange two different coins without a third-party intermediary, usually an exchange, and without needing to buy or sell. Centralized exchanges, such as Coinbase, cannot perform atomic swaps. Instead, decentralized exchanges allow for atomic swaps and give full control to end users.

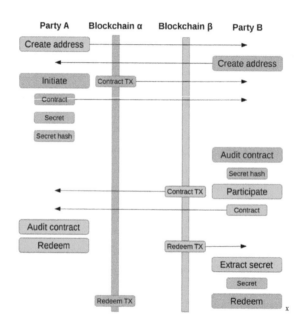

*Visualization of an Atomic Swap Workflow.

What are Bitcoin mining pools?

Mining pools, also known as group mining, refers to groups of people or entities who combine their computational power to mine together and split the rewards. This also ensures consistent earnings since rewards are otherwise infrequent and pools allow for such rewards to be combined and evenly distributed on a regular (typically every-few-hours) basis.

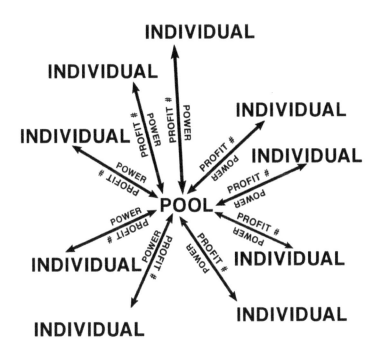

Who are the largest Bitcoin miners?

The following visual is a breakdown of Bitcoin miner distribution. The large chunks are all mining pools, not individual miners, since pools enable massive scale (in terms of computational power) by leveraging a vast network of individuals. This, in essence, applies the very Bitcoin-like concept of distribution to mining. The largest Bitcoin pools include Antpool (an open-access mining pool) ViaBTC (known for being safe and stable), Slush Pool (the oldest mining pool) and BTC.com (the largest of the four).

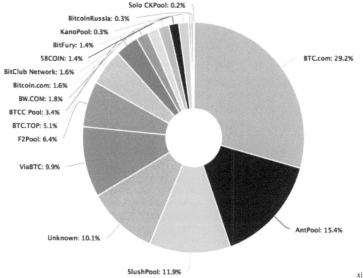

Is Bitcoin technology outdated?

Yes, the technology powering Bitcoin is outdated relative to newer competitors. Bitcoin did the work of trailblazing and acted as a proof-of-concept for cryptocurrencies, but as with all technology, innovation pushes forwards and keeping up with such innovation requires cohesive and major upgrades, which Bitcoin hasn't had. The Bitcoin network can handle about 7 transactions per second, while Ethereum (the second-largest cryptocurrency by market cap) can handle 30 transactions per second and Cardano, the third largest and much newer cryptocurrency, can handle about 1 million transactions per second. Network congestion on the Bitcoin network leads to higher fees, and in this way, as well as in programmability, privacy, and energy use, Bitcoin is somewhat outdated. This doesn't mean it doesn't work; it does, it just means either serious upgrades should be implemented, or user experience will worsen, and competitors will thrive over time. Regardless, Bitcoin has enormous brand value, a massive scale of usage and adoption, and protocols that get the job done in a secure manner. We'll likely see neither the best (large upgrades that solve all the problems) nor worst (too outdated, no longer works, and goes to zero) situation play out; instead, the middle ground is likely, in which Bitcoin continues to face problems, continues to implement solutions, and continues to grow (although growth will have to slow at some point) as the crypto space grows.

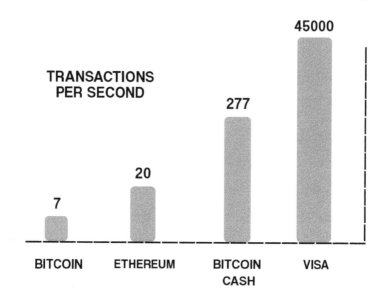

Note the transactions per second as a function of Bitcoin's relative

advancement.

Are there multiple types of nodes?

A node is a computer (any computer, not a specific type) connected to a blockchain's network. Such computers assist the blockchain in writing and validating blocks by solving mathematical equations (see questions on hashing) and performing other tasks. Some nodes download an entire history of their blockchain; these are called masternodes and perform more tasks than regular nodes. Additionally, nodes are in no way tied to a specific network; nodes can switch to many different blockchains practically at will, as is the case with multipool mining.

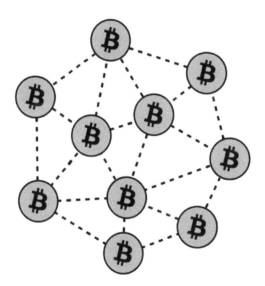

How does the supply mechanism of Bitcoin work?

Bitcoin uses a PoW supply mechanism. A supply mechanism is the way in which new tokens are introduced onto the network. PoW, or "Proof of work," literally means that work (in terms of mathematical equations) is required to create blocks. The people who do the work are miners.

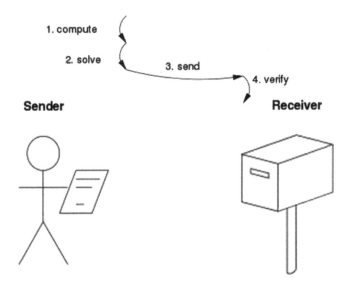

*Transactions are computed and solved by miners, verified, and confirmed.

How is the market cap of Bitcoin calculated?

The equation for market cap is very simple: # of units x price per unit.
Bitcoin "units" are coins, so to solve for market cap one may multiply the
circulating supply (approx.18.8 million) by the price per coin (approx.
$50,000). The resulting number (in this case, 940 billion) is the market
cap. The following visual displays the top cryptocurrencies by market cap
(from assetdash.com)

(NUMBER OF UNITS) (PRICE PER UNIT) = MARKET CAP

Asset Name	Symbol	Market Cap	Price	Today
Bitcoin	BTC	$898,620,560,264	$47,746.55	-0.97%
Ethereum	ETH	$395,784,687,227	$3,365.78	-2.16%
Cardano	ADA	$75,259,032,949	$2.35	-0.92%
Binance Coin	BNB	$70,067,898,552	$416.73	1.32%
Tether	USDT	$68,370,433,747	$1.001141	0.17%
XRP	XRP	$49,875,925,952	$1.069788	-0.57%
Solana	SOL	$46,926,947,343	$158.02	-3.47%
Polkadot	DOT	$34,097,572,182	$34.53	-0.61%

Can you give and get Bitcoin loans?

Yes, you can leverage Bitcoin and other cryptocurrencies to take out a USD loan. Such loans are ideal for people who don't want to sell their Bitcoin holdings, but need money for expenses such as car or property payments, traveling, buying a property, etc. Taking out a loan allows the holder to maintain ownership of their assets, yet still take advantage of the value locked in such assets. Additionally, Bitcoin loans have extremely fast turnaround and acceptance times, credit scores are irrelevant, and loans come with some degree of confidentiality (meaning, lenders have no interest in what you spend the money on). As a lender, it's a good strategy to create income from otherwise sedentary holdings; on both sides, the risk is largely in the fluctuations of Bitcoin. The most popular services to give and get Bitcoin and coin loans are blockfi.com, lendabit, youhodler, bitpops, coinloan.io, and mycred.io.

What are the largest problems with Bitcoin?

Bitcoin, unfortunately, is not perfect; especially being the first of its kind (and more of an experiment than anything else). The largest current and long-term problem facing Bitcoin is that of energy and scale. Bitcoin operates through a PoW (proof-of-work) system, and the incurred downside is high energy usage; Bitcoin currently uses 78 TW/hour per year (much of which, though not all, utilizes carbon). To provide some perspective, a terawatt-hour is a unity of energy equal to outputting one trillion watts for one hour. Despite this, the Bitcoin network consumes three times less energy than the traditional money system; the issue lies in the energy usage at mass adoption and the energy use relative to other cryptocurrencies. A PoS (proof-of-stake) system, such as that soon to be employed by Ethereum, uses 99.95% less energy than a PoW alternative.[xii] This is more important than any absolute energy consumption data, because it hints at the fact that Bitcoin has the potential to consume much less energy than it currently does. In addition to scale and energy, an equally important problem facing Bitcoin in the long run (not in terms of survival, but in terms of value) is utility. Bitcoin has little inherent utility and serves more as a store of value than a technology. It could be argued that Bitcoin fills a niche and acts like a digital gold, but the double-edged sword of such a niche is that Bitcoin's volatility is extremely high for a long-term store of value. At some point, either the volatility must decrease, or usage will remain limited to the demographic that is comfortable with high volatility. At the very least, the question of utility does bring up the question of altcoin alternatives; since the use cases of cryptocurrencies are varied, especially regarding utility, and therefore cryptocurrencies other than Bitcoin must and will exist at scale in the long run. The question of which one, if answered correctly, will be very profitable.

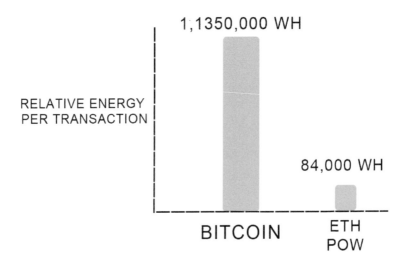

Does Bitcoin have coins or tokens?

Bitcoin consists of coins; that said, one should understand the difference between a token and a coin. A cryptocurrency token is a digital unit that represents an asset, just like a coin. However, while coins are built upon their own blockchain, tokens are built upon another blockchain. Many tokens use the Ethereum blockchain, and are thus referred to as tokens, not coins. Coins are mostly used only as money, while tokens have a wider range of uses (as a technology). Understanding tokens is an integral part of understanding exactly what you're trading, as well as understanding all uses of digital currencies, and for those reasons the most popular token subcategories are analyzed here:

Security tokens represent legal ownership of an asset, whether digital or physical. The word "security" in security tokens isn't security as in being safe, but rather "security" as referring to any financial instrument that holds value and can be traded. Basically, security tokens represent an investment or asset.

Utility tokens are built into an existing protocol and can access the services of that protocol. Protocols provide rules and a structure for nodes to follow, and utility tokens can be used for wider purposes than purely as a payment token. For example, utility tokens are commonly given to investors during an ICO. Then, later, investors can use the utility tokens they received as a means of payment on the platform they received the tokens from. Generally, utility tokens, as the name implies, do more than exist as a means of value through some function of utility.

Governance tokens are used to create and run a voting system for cryptocurrencies that allows for system upgrades without a centralized owner.

Payment (transactional) tokens are solely used to pay for goods and services.

Can you earn money just by holding Bitcoin?

Many coins will provide rewards just for holding the asset; Ethereum holders will soon make 5% APR (annually) on staked ETH. However, the keyword is "staked" since coins that offer rewards just for holding the coin or token (called "staking rewards") mostly operate on a PoS (proof-of-stake) system and algorithm. A PoS algorithm is an alternative to PoW that allows a person to mine and validate transactions based on the number of units held. So, with PoS, the more you own, the more you mine. Ethereum may soon run on proof-of-stake, and many alternatives already do. All that said, you still can earn interest on Bitcoin by lending it out to borrowers (refer to: Can I get loans for my Bitcoin?).

Crypto*	Price ($)*	Staked Amount*	% Staked*	Average Staking Reward**
Cardano (ADA)	$1.13	$25.85B	72.88%	5.47%
Polkadot (DOT)	$37.43	$25.59B	64.22%	9.82%
Ethereum 2.0 (ETH)	$1,804.52	$6.17B	2.95%	14.00%
Algorand (ALGO)	$1.11	$5.40B	57.13%	7.96%
Solana (SOL)	$14.49	$3.68B	51.62%	17.30%
Cosmos (ATOM)	$19.51	$3.56B	67.11%	9.62%
Terra (LUNA)	$10.92	$3.42B	32.22%	7.03%
Avalanche (AVAX)	$31.60	$2.94B	24.44%	14.25%
Tezos (XTZ)	$4.14	$2.86B	78.03%	5.79%
Dai (DAI)	$1.00	$2.832B	n/a	8.27% [xiii]

*Average staking rewards of top PoS cryptocurrencies. Visuals and data from coinmarketexpert.com and stakingrewards.com

Does Bitcoin have slippage?

To provide some context, slippage can occur when a trade is placed through a market order. Market orders execute at the best possible price, but sometimes a notable difference between the expected price and actual price occurs. For example, you may see that JB is at $100 a coin, so you put in a market order for $1000. However, you end up only getting 9.8 JB for your $1000, as opposed to the expected 10. Slippage happens because bid/ask spreads change quickly; basically, the market price of the asset changed after the order was placed and before the order executed. Bitcoin and most cryptocurrencies are liable to slippage; for this reason, if you're placing a large order, it's best to place a limit order as opposed to a market order.

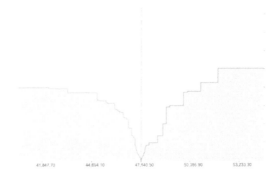

41,847.70   44,694.10   47,540.50   50,386.90   53,233.30

* Depth charts convey information about the market price of an asset, bids, and asks.

What Bitcoin acronyms should I know?

ATH

Acronym meaning "all-time high." This is the highest price a cryptocurrency reaches within a chosen period.

ATL

Acronym meaning "all-time low." This is the lowest price a cryptocurrency reaches within a chosen period.

BTD

Acronym meaning "Buy the Dip." May also be represented, along with some salty language, as BTFD.

CEX

Acronym meaning "centralized exchange." Centralized exchanges are owned by a company that manages trading. Coinbase is a popular CEX.

ICO

"Initial coin offering."

P2P

"Peer to peer."

PND

"Pump and dump."

DLT

Acronym meaning "Distributed Ledger Technology." A distributed ledger is stored in many different locations so transactions can be validated by multiple parties. Blockchain networks use distributed ledgers.

SATS

SATS is shorthand for Satoshi Nakamoto, which is the pseudonym used by the creator of Bitcoin. A SATS is the smallest allowed unit of bitcoin, which is 0.00000001 BTC. The smallest unit of bitcoin is also referred to as a Satoshi. If Bitcoin hits $1 million per coin, each Satoshi would be worth 1 US cent.

What Bitcoin slang should I know?

Bag

A bag refers to one's position. If you own a sizable quantity in a coin, you own a bag of them.

Bag Holder

A bag holder is a trader who has a position in a worthless coin.

Dolphin

Crypto holders are classified through several different animals. Those with extremely large holdings (eight figures and up) are called whales, while those with moderately sized holdings are called dolphins.

Flippening / Flappening

The "flippening" is used to describe the hypothetical moment when, if at all, Etherium (ETH) passes Bitcoin (BTC) in market cap. The "flappening" was the moment when Litecoin (LTC) passed Bitcoin Cash (BCH) in market cap. The flappening happened in 2018, while the flippening has yet to occur, and based purely on market cap, is unlikely to ever happen.

Moon / To the Moon

Terms such as "to the moon" and "it's going to the moon" simply refer to cryptocurrency going up in value, typically by an extreme amount.

Vaporware

Vaporware is a coin or token that has been hyped up but has little intrinsic value and is thus likely to decrease in value.

Vladimir Club

A term that describes someone who has acquired 1% of 1% (0.01%) of the maximum supply of a cryptocurrency. To be in the Bitcoin Vladimir Club, one must own (as of the current market cap) $90 million of BTC.

Weak Hands

Traders who have "weak hands" lack confidence to hold assets in the face of volatility; such traders largely trade on emotion, as opposed to sticking to a trading plan.

REKT

Phonetic spelling of "wrecked."

HODL

"Hold on for dear life."

DYOR

"Do your own research."

FOMO

"Fear of missing out."

FUD

"Fear, uncertainty and doubt."

JOMO

"Joy of missing out."

ELI5

"Explain it like I'm 5."

Can you use leverage or margin to trade Bitcoin?

To provide context for those not familiar with leveraged trading, traders can "leverage" trading power by trading on borrowed funds from a third party. For example, say you have $1,000 and you're using 5x leverage; you're now trading with $5,000 worth of funds, $4,000 of which you borrowed. By that same function, 10x leverage is $10,000 and 100x is $100,000. Leverage allows you to amplify profits by using money that isn't yours and keeping some of the extra profit. Margin trading is almost interchangeable with leverage trading (since margin creates leverage) and the only difference is that margin is expressed as a percentage deposit required, while leverage is a ratio (meaning, you may margin trade at 3x leverage). Leverage and margin trading is very risky; generally speaking, unless you're an experienced trader and you have some financial stability, leverage trading is not recommended. That said, many exchanges do offer leveraged trading services for Bitcoin and other cryptocurrencies. The following lists the best crypto leverage trading services.

Leverage Trading Resources:

- Binance (popular, best overall)
- Bybit (best charts)
- BitMEX (easiest to use)
- Deribit (best for leveraged Bitcoin trading)
- Kraken (popular, user friendly)
- Poloniex (high liquidity)

Take note of how leveraged investing enables large returns; as exemplified in this case, more risk equals more reward.

The Power of Leverage				
Leverage	Capital Invested	Purchase Power	Money Value of 1% Profit	ROI
2:1	$1000	$2000	$20	2%
10:1	$1000	$10,000	$100	10%
50:1	$1000	$50,000	$500	50%
100:1	$1000	$100,000	$1,000	100%
150:1	$1000	$150,000	$1,500	150%
200:1	$1000	$200,000	$2,000	200%

xiv

What is support and resistance for Bitcoin?

Here, we delve into technical analysis and the trading of Bitcoin. Support is the price of a coin or token at which that asset is less likely to go below since many people are willing to buy the asset at that price. Often, if a coin hits support levels, it will reverse into an uptrend. This is usually a good time to buy the coin, although if the price falls beneath the support level, the coin is likely to fall further down to a lower support level. Resistance, on the other hand, is a price that an asset finds difficult to break through since many people find that a good price to at which to sell. Sometimes, levels of resistance can be psychological. For example, Bitcoin might hit resistance at $50,000, since many people were thinking "when bitcoin hits $50,000, I will sell." Often, when a resistance level is broken through, price can quickly climb. For example, if bitcoin did break past $50,000, the price might quickly climb to $55,000, at which time it may face more resistance, and $50,000 may then become the new support level.

Support and resistance visual.

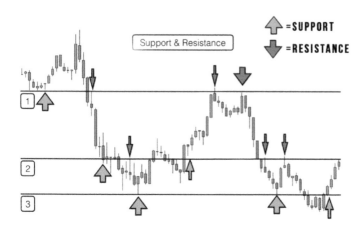

xv

Note that resistance incurs price pullbacks, and support incurs price rebounds.

Who owns Bitcoin?

The idea that Bitcoin is "owned" is correct in only the most distributed sense. About 20 million people collectively own all the bitcoin in the world, but Bitcoin itself, as a network, cannot be owned.[4]

Active Crypto Traders Across The Globe

xvi

*A 2019 study by CH&Co found that about 43 million active crypto traders exist. Of these, 20 million collectively own all bitcoins.

How do you read a Bitcoin chart?

This is a grand question; to answer, the following section will aim to break down the most popular types of charts used to read Bitcoin and other cryptocurrencies, as well as how to read such charts. The following different types of charts and respective uses will be broken down:

- Line Chart
- Candlestick Chart
- Renko Chart
- Point & Figure Chart
- Heiken-Ashi Chart

Line Chart

A line chart is a chart that represents price through one single line. Most charts are line charts because such charts are extremely easy to understand, although the flip side of this is that they contain less information than popular alternatives. Robinhood and Coinbase (both of which target their services towards less experienced investors) have line charts as the default chart type, while institutions aimed towards a more experienced audience, such as Charles Schwab and Binance, use other chart forms as default.

Line Chart – *tradingview.com*

Candlestick Chart

Candlestick charts are a much more useful form of displaying information about a coin; such charts are the chart of choice for most investors. Within a given period, candlestick charts have a wide "real body" and are most often represented as red or green (another common color scheme is empty/white and filled/black real bodies). If it is red (or filled in), the closing price was lower than the opening price (meaning it went down). If the real body is green (or empty), the close was higher than the open (meaning it went up). Above and below the real bodies are the "wicks" also known as "shadows." Wicks show the high and low prices of the period's trading. So, combining what we know, if the upper wick (aka the upper shadow) is close to the real body, the high the coin or token reached during the day was near the closing price. Hence, the opposite also applies. Understanding and taking advantage of candlestick charts are essential to reach any degree of investing competency.

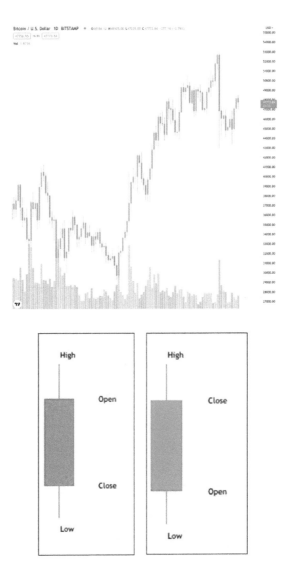

Candlestick images source – tradingview.com

Renko Chart

Renko charts only show price movement and ignore time and volume. Renko comes from the Japanese term "renga," meaning "bricks." Renko charts use bricks (also known as boxes), typically red/green or white/black. Renko boxes only form at the top or bottom right corner of the proceeding box, and the next box can only form if the price passes the top or bottom of the previous box. For example, if the predefined amount is $1 (think of this as similar to time intervals on candlestick charts), then the next box can only form once it passes either $1 above or $1 below the price of the previous box. These charts simplify and "smooth out" trends into easy-to-understand patterns while removing random price action. This can make conducting technical analysis easier since patterns such as support and resistance levels are much more blatantly displayed.

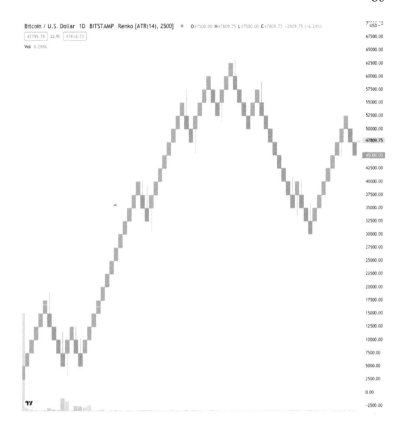

Renko Chart – *tradingview.com*

Point & Figure Chart

While point and figure (P&F) charts aren't as well-known as the others on this list, they do have a long history and a reputation as one of the simplest charts used to identify good entry and exit points. Like Renko charts, P&F charts don't directly account for the passage of time. Rather, X's and O's are stacked in columns; each letter represents a chosen price movement (just like the blocks in Renko charts). X's represent a rising price, and O's represent a falling price. Look at this sequence:

X

X O X

X O

X

Let's say the chosen price movement is $10. We must start at the bottom left: the 3 X's indicate that the price rose $30, the 2 O's signify a $20 drop, and then the final 2 X's represent a $20 rise. Time, again, is irrelevant.

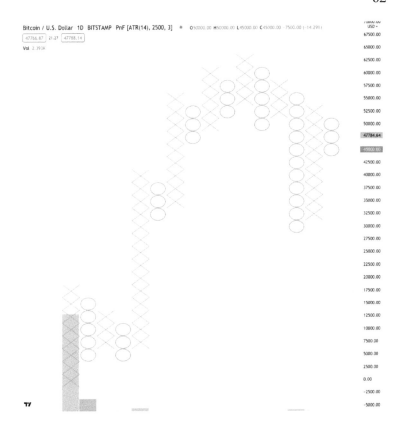

Point & Figure Chart – *tradingview.com*

Heiken-Ashi Chart

Heikin-Ashi (hik-in-aw-she) charts are a simpler, smoothed out version of candlestick charts. They function almost the same way as candlestick charts, (candles, wicks, shadows, etc.), except HA charts spread price data over two periods instead of one. This, essentially, makes Heikin-Ashi preferable to many traders versus candlestick charts because patterns and trends can be more easily spotted, and false signals (small, meaningless moves) are, in large part, omitted. That said, the simpler appearance does obscure some data relative to candlesticks, which is partly why Heikin-Ashis hasn't yet replaced candlesticks. So, I suggest that you experiment with both chart types and figure out which best fits your style and ability to discern trends.

Heiken-Ashi Chart – *tradingview.com*

Note that the trends on the Heikin-Ashi chart are smoother and thus more discernible than on the candlestick chart.

Charting Resources

TradingView

tradingview.com (best overall, best social)

CoinMarketCap

coinmarketcap.com (simple, easy)

CryptoWatch

cryptowat.ch (very established, best for bots)

CryptoView

cryptoview.com (very customizable)

Chart Pattern Classifications

Chart patterns are classified to help a viewer understand the information a given pattern is meant to convey. Here are a few of such classifications:

Bullish

Bullish patterns are likely to result in the outcome being favorable to the upside. For example, a bullish pattern may result in a 10% gain.

Bearish

All bearish patterns are likely to result in the outcome being favorable to the downside, so for example, a bearish pattern may result in a 10% downtrend.

Candlestick

Candlestick patterns apply specifically to candlestick charts, not to all charts. This is because candlestick patterns rely on information that can only come across in a candle (body and wick) format.

Number of Bars/Candles

The number of bars or candles in a pattern is usually no more than three.

Continuation

Continuation patterns signal that the pre-pattern trend is more likely than not to continue. So, for example, if continuation pattern X forms at the top of an uptrend, then the uptrend is likely to continue.

Breakout

A breakout is a move above resistance or below support. Breakout patterns indicate that such a move is probable. The direction of that breakout is specific to the pattern.

Reversal

A reversal is a change in the direction of price. A reversal pattern indicates that the direction of the price is likely to change (so, an uptrend would become a downtrend, and a downtrend would become an uptrend).

What is a Bitcoin bubble?

A bubble in Bitcoin and all investments refers to a time during which value is rising at an unsustainable rate. Often, bubbles will pop and trigger a large crash. For this reason, being in a bubble, whether referring to the market as a whole or a specific coin or token, is both a good and (more so) a bad thing. The below visuals are the phases of a bubble, as envisioned by Jean-Paul Rodrigue, a Canadian scholar.

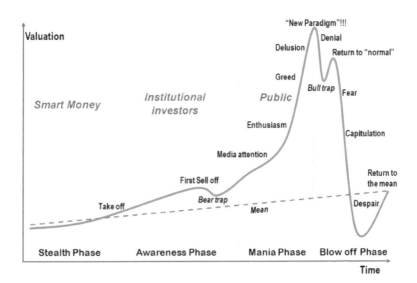

What does "bullish" and "bearish" mean for Bitcoin?

To be a bear means that you think the price of a coin, token, or the value of the entire market is going to go down. If you think like this, you're also considered "bearish" on the given security. The opposite is to be bullish: a person who thinks a security will rise in value is bullish on that security. These words were popularized in stock market terminology, and the origin is thought to be tied to the traits of the animals: a bull will thrust its horns upwards while attacking an opponent, while a bear will stand up and swipe down.

Is Bitcoin cyclical?

Yes, Bitcoin is historically cyclical and tends to operate on multi-year cycles (specifically, 4-year cycles) that tend to have the following pattern: breakthrough highs, a correction, accumulation, and recovery and continuation. This can be simplified into a big up, major down, little up or sideways, and a big up. Breakthrough highs typically follow (normally a year or so after) Bitcoin's halving events, which happen every four years (the most recent of which occurred in 2020). This, by no means, is an exact science, but it does provide some perspective on the medium-term potential and price action of Bitcoin. Additionally, large jumps of Altcoins (specifically medium and small altcoins) typically occur while Bitcoin is neither making a major upwards move nor a major downwards move, and often following a large upward move. At such a point, investors take Bitcoin profits (while the price consolidates) and put them into smaller coins. So, all this is generally something to think about, especially if you're thinking about buying or selling Bitcoin as opposed to holding.

What is Bitcoin's utility?

Utility within a coin or token is one of the most important aspects of due diligence since understanding the current and long-term utility and value behind a coin or token allows for a much clearer analysis of potential. Utility is defined as being useful and functional; crypto coins or tokens with utility have real, practical uses. They don't just exist but rather serve to solve a problem or offer a service. Coins with the most functional current uses and use cases are likely to succeed as opposed to those without continued purpose, use, and innovation. Here are a few case studies, including that of Bitcoin:

❖ Bitcoin (BTC) serves as a reliable and long-term store of value, akin to "digital gold."

❖ Ethereum (ETH) allows for the creation of dApps and Smart Contracts on top of the Ethereum blockchain.

❖ Storj (STORJ) can be used to store data in the cloud in a decentralized manner, kin to Google Drive and Dropbox.

❖ Basic Attention Token (BAT) is used within the Brave browser to earn rewards and send tips to creators.

❖ Golem (GNT) is a global supercomputer that offers rentable computing resources in exchange for GNT tokens.

Is it better to hold Bitcoin or trade it?

Historically speaking, it is more profitable and easier to simply hold Bitcoin. The time, effort, and timing required to trade successfully (or to turn a greater profit than those who hold) is an enormously difficult mixture to assemble; those who do it are usually full-time traders or have access to tools that others don't. Unless you're willing to embrace this level of dedication or you truly enjoy the process, you're much better off buying and holding Bitcoin for the long-term.

Bitcoin monthly returns

	Jan	Feb	Mar	April	May	June	July	Aug	Sept	Oct	Nov	Dec
2011	75%	22%	-15%	352%	182%	68%	-13%	-37%	-38%	-35%	-6%	53%
2012	5%	-20%	-1%	3%	4%	27%	41%	6%	24%	-10%	19%	8%
2013	54%	63%	171%	34%	10%	-31%	18%	33%	-3%	59%	451%	-24%
2014	7%	-32%	-20%	-6%	36%	1%	-9%	-20%	-18%	-12%	17%	-15%
2015	-31%	12%	-6%	-4%	-1%	18%	10%	-18%	4%	32%	14%	19%
2016	-16%	18%	-4%	8%	17%	25%	-8%	-6%	6%	14%	2%	29%
2017	-3%	20%	-12%	27%	60%	2%	19%	74%	-12%	47%	49%	29%
2018	-25%	14%	-37%	36%	-18%	-15%	21%	-8%	-8%	-4%	-37%	-11%
2019	-10%	63%	7%	27%	61%	27%	-5%	-8%	-15%	10%	-18%	-5%
2020	30%	-9%	-25%	35%	10%	-3%	24%	3%	-8%	28%	43%	47%
2021	15%	48%										

data: tradingview.com xvii

Is investing in Bitcoin risky?

The below image is based on the risk-return trade-off principle. When one sees everyone else making money (as is largely and dangerously enabled by social media, since everyone posts the wins and not the losses), as is currently happening in the crypto market, we're prone to subconsciously (or consciously) assume a lack of significant risk. However, generally speaking (especially regarding investments), the more reward there is, the more risk there is. Investing in cryptocurrencies is not risk-free, nor low risk; it is extremely risky, but being a double-edged sword, it also offers extreme reward.

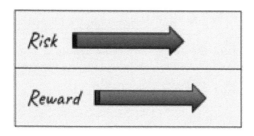

What is the Bitcoin white paper?

A white paper is an informational report issued by an organization about a given product, service, or general idea. White papers explain (really, sell) the concept and provide an idea and timetable of future events. Generally, this helps readers understand a problem, figure out how the creators of the paper aim to solve that problem, and form an opinion about that project. Three types of white papers frequent the business space: first, the "backgrounder," which explains the background behind a product, service, or idea and provides technical, education-focused information that sells the reader. A second type of white paper is a "numbered list" which displays content in a digestible, number-oriented format. For example, "10 use cases for coin CM" or "10 reasons token HL will dominate the market." A final type is a problem/solution white paper, which defines the problem that the product, service, or idea aims to solve, and explains the created solution.

White papers are used within the crypto space to explain novel concepts and the technicalities, vision, and plans surrounding a given project. All professional crypto projects will have a white paper, typically found on their website. Reading the white paper gives you a better understanding of a project than practically any other single source of accessible information. Bitcoin's white paper was published in 2008 and outlined the principles of a transparent and uncontrollable cryptographically secure, distributed, and P2P electronic payment system. You can read the original Bitcoin white paper for yourself at the following link:

bitcoin.org/bitcoin.pdf

Below are a few websites that provide more information about, or access to, cryptocurrency white papers.

All Crypto White Papers - https://www.allcryptowhitepapers.com

CryptoRating - https://cryptorating.eu/whitepapers

What are Bitcoin keys?

A key is a random string of characters used by algorithms to encrypt data. Bitcoin and most cryptocurrencies use two keys: a public key and a private key. Both keys are strings of letters and numbers. New users receive a pair of a public key and a private key; the public key is used to receive cryptocurrencies, while the private key allows the user to carry out transactions from within their account. Both keys are stored in a wallet.

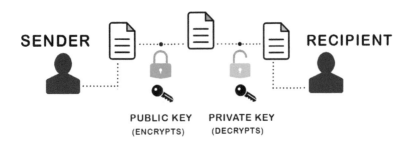

Is Bitcoin scarce?

Yes. Bitcoin is a deflationary asset with a fixed supply. Fixed-supply cryptocurrencies have an algorithmic supply limit. Bitcoin, as mentioned, is a fixed-supply asset, since no more coins can possibly be created once 21 million have been put into circulation. Currently, nearly 90% of bitcoins have been mined and around 0.5% of the total supply is being removed from circulation per year due to coins being sent to inaccessible accounts. As per halving (covered later on), Bitcoin will hit its maximum supply around the year 2140. Many other cryptocurrencies, such as Binance Coin (BNB), Cardano (ADA), Litecoin (LTC), and ChainLink (LINK), are also founded upon a fixed-supply, deflationary system. Further information on the concept of deflationary systems and why this makes Bitcoin scarce is outlined in the, "What does Bitcoin being deflationary mean?" question below.

What are Bitcoin whales?

Whales, in cryptocurrency, refer to individuals or entities that hold enough of a given coin or token to be considered major players with the potential to influence price action. Around 1000 individual Bitcoin whales own 40% of all bitcoins, and 13% of all bitcoins are held in just over 100 accounts.[5] Bitcoin whales can manipulate the price of Bitcoin through various strategies, and certainly have in recent years. An interesting article on a related subject matter (published by Medium) is titled "Bitcoin Whales and Crypto Market Manipulation."[xviii]

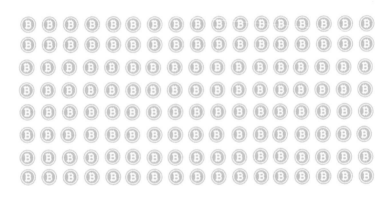

Who are Bitcoin miners?

Bitcoin miners are anyone who lends computational power to the Bitcoin network. This ranges from Nicehash PC users to complete mining farms; anyone who adds any power to the network (thus increasing the hash rate) is defined as a miner. Bitcoin miners offer computational power to the Bitcoin network, which is used to verify transactions and add blocks to the blockchain, in return for rewards in Bitcoin.

What does it mean to "burn" Bitcoin?

The term "burn" refers to the process of burning, which is a supply mechanism that enables coins to be taken out of circulation, hence acting as a deflationary tool and increasing the value of each other coin in the network (the concept of which is much like a company buying back stock in the stock market). Burning can be performed in several different ways: one of these ways is sending coins to an inaccessible wallet, which is called an "eater address." In this case, while the tokens haven't technically been removed from the total supply, the circulating supply has effectively gone down. Currently, around 3.7 million Bitcoins (200+ billion of value) have been lost through this process. Tokens can also be burned by coding a burn function into the protocols that govern a token, but the far more used method is through the mentioned eater addresses. A cryptocurrency analyst named Timothy Paterson has asserted that 1,500 Bitcoins are lost each day, which far exceed the average daily increase (through mining) of 900. Ultimately, to a point, the loss of coins increases scarcity and value and is therefore a positive force for investors.

What does it mean that Bitcoin is inflationary?

Bitcoin is a fixed-supply asset (meaning coin supply has an algorithmic limit) since no more coins can possibly be created once 21 million have been put into circulation. Currently, nearly 90% of Bitcoins have been mined, and around 0.5% of the total supply is being lost per year. As a result of halving, Bitcoin will hit its maximum supply around 2140. The most apparent benefit of a fixed and max-supply system is that such systems are deflationary. Deflationary assets are assets in which the total supply decreases over time, and therefore each unit increases in value. For example, say you're stranded on a desert island with 10 other people, and each person has 1 bottle of water. Since some people will presumably drink their water, the total supply of 100 bottles of water can only decrease. This makes the water a deflationary asset. As total supply shrinks, each water bottle becomes worth increasingly more. Say, now, there are only 20 water bottles left. Each of the 20 water bottles is worth as much as 5 water bottles were once worth when all 100 were being circulated. In this way, long-term holders of deflationary assets experience an increase in value of their holdings because the fundamental value relative to the whole (in the water-bottle example, 1 bottle out of 100 is 1%, while 1 out of 20 is 5%, making each bottle worth 5x more) has increased. Overall, a fixed-supply and deflationary model, much like digital gold (especially regarding Bitcoin specifically), will increase the fundamental value of each coin or token over time and create value through scarcity.

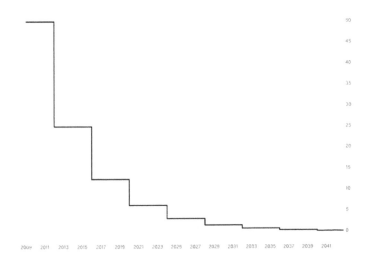

This visual displays the number of coins added to the network each year. In 2009, 50 coins were mined every 10 minutes. Now, in 2021, 6.25 coins are mined every ten minutes, and this number will continue to halve every four years.

What is Bitcoin's volume?

Trading volume, known just as "volume," is the number of coins or tokens traded within a specified time frame. Volume can show the relative health of a certain coin or the overall market. For example, Bitcoin (BTC) currently has a 24h volume of $46 billion, while Litecoin (LTC), within the same timeframe, trades $7 billion. This number itself, however, is somewhat arbitrary; a standardized means of comparison within volume is the ratio between the market cap and the volume. For example, continuing with the two coins above, Bitcoin has a market cap of $1.1 trillion and a volume of $46 billion, meaning that $1 in every $24 on the network was traded in the past 24 hours. Yet, Litecoin has a market cap of $16.7 billion and a 24h volume of $7 billion, meaning that $1 of every $2.3 on the network was traded in the past 24 hours. Through an understanding of volume, other information about a coin, such as popularity, volatility, utility, and so on, can be better understood. Information on the volume of cryptocurrencies can be found below:

CoinMarketCap - *coinmarketcap.com*

CoinGecko – *coingecko.com*

How is Bitcoin mined?

Bitcoin is mined through the application of nodes (nodes, to recap, are computers in the network). Nodes solve complex hashing problems, and owners of nodes are rewarded in proportion to the amount of work (hence, proof-of-work) completed. In this way, the owners of nodes (called miners) can mine Bitcoin.

Servers generate complex math problems.

↓

Computers solve the problems.

↓

When the problems are solved, bitcoins are released.

↓

The bitcoins are given to the owner(s) of the computer(s) that solved the problem.

Can you get USD with Bitcoin?

Yes! Fiat currencies can be converted into and out of Bitcoin through a fiat-to-crypto pair. In the question directly below, you'll learn about pairs. The Bitcoin-to-USD pair is BTC/USD. US dollars are the quoted currency for Bitcoin and other currencies, which means USD is the yardstick to which other cryptocurrencies are compared; this is why you may say, "Bitcoin hits 50,000" while Bitcoin really arrived at a value equivalent to 50,000 US dollars. As can be seen in the below visual, Bitcoin and other cryptocurrencies are exchangeable for quite a few fiat currencies, and practically all cryptocurrencies are exchangeable for Bitcoin. Therefore, practically all cryptocurrencies may be exchanged for all common fiat currencies through several degrees of transaction.

BTC to USD	ETH to USD	XRP to USD
BTC to AUD	ETH to AUD	XRP to AUD
BTC to BRL	ETH to BRL	XRP to BRL
BTC to CNY	ETH to CNY	XRP to CNY
BTC to GBP	ETH to GBP	XRP to GBP
BTC to INR	ETH to INR	XRP to INR
BTC to JPY	ETH to JPY	XRP to JPY
BTC to KRW	ETH to KRW	XRP to KRW
BTC to RUB	ETH to RUB	XRP to RUB

What is a Bitcoin pair?

All cryptocurrencies operate in pairs. A pair is a combination of two cryptocurrencies that allows for such cryptos to be exchanged. A BTC/ETH (crypto-to-crypto) pair allows Bitcoin to be exchanged for Ethereum, and vice versa. A BTC/USD (crypto-to-fiat) pair allows Bitcoin to exchange for the US Dollar, and vice versa. Given the large number of smaller cryptocurrencies, the exchange market is built around a few large cryptocurrencies that, in turn, exchange into everything. For example, a Celo (CGLD) to Fetch.ai (FET) pair may not exist, but a CGLD/BTC and a BTC/FET pair allows CGLD to be converted into FET. Put simply, pairs are the web that connects different assets, while we're all the spiders. Pairs also allow for arbitrage, which is trading on the difference in pair prices between different exchanges and markets. Below are the current most active cryptocurrency pairs, as per data from investing.com.

Name :	Exchange :	Last
SHIB/USD	Huobi	0.00000701
SHIB/INR	Bitbns	0.000569
Dogecoin	Investing.com	0.202946
TRX/USD	Binance	0.09002
DOGE/USD	Binance	0.202800
VET/USD	Binance	0.089980
XRP	Investing.com	0.92867
Cardano	Investing.com	2.0564

Is Bitcoin better than Ethereum?

The key difference between Bitcoin and Ethereum is the value proposition. Bitcoin was created as a store of value, kin to a digital gold, while Ethereum acts as a platform through which decentralized applications (dApps) and smart contracts can be created and powered by the ETH token and the Solidity programming language. Since ETH is needed to run dApps on the Ethereum blockchain, the value of ETH is somewhat tied to utility. In one sentence: Bitcoin is a currency while Ethereum is a technology, and in this regard Ethereum wasn't created as a competitor to Bitcoin, but rather to complement and build alongside it. For this, the question of which is better is like comparing an apple to a brick; both are great at what they do and choosing one coin over the other is choosing one value proposition over the other (for example: we need the apple for food, but the brick to create shelter). The question of which, ultimately, does not have a clear or agreed-upon answer.

Can you buy things with Bitcoin?

Bitcoin represents a shared sense of value; value can be transacted and exchanged for equivalent value, just like any other currency. Despite this, it's quite difficult to directly buy most things with Bitcoin, although options do exist and are rapidly expanding. Of course, one may always just exchange Bitcoin for their given currency and use such currency to buy things, but the question remains: why can you not yet use Bitcoin to purchase any items you would otherwise pay for with other digital payment methods? Such a question is complex, but mostly has to do with the fact that the established system of government-backed currencies has worked for quite a while, while cryptocurrencies are new, have yet to integrate into commercial systems, and operate outside of government control. Current trends point to cryptocurrencies integrating to a much greater extent into online (and offline) retailers, wholesalers, and independent sellers. Already, Microsoft (in the Xbox store), Home Depot (via Flexa), Starbucks (via Bakkt), Whole Foods (via Spedn), and many other companies accept Bitcoin; the tipping points are whether or when the major online retailers start accepting Bitcoin (Amazon, Walmart, Target, etc) and the point at which governments either embrace or push back against cryptocurrencies as a payment method. The following lists companies, which, at the very least at some time or in some locations, have allowed Bitcoin as a payment method. Data is sourced from icoholder.com and is extremely liable to change.

• Alzashop.com	• OKCupid
• Archive.org	• Overstock.com
• Badoo.com	• Paypal
• BigFishGames.com	• PizzaForCoins.com
• Menlo Park	• Rakutan
• Bitcoincoffee.com	• Red Cross
• Bloomberg.com	• Reddit
• Braintree	• Seoclerks.com
• CheapAir.com	• Shopify.com
• Crowdtilt.com	• Stripe
• Dish Network	• Subway
• Domino's Pizza	• The Pirate Bay
• eGifter.com	• Virgin Galactic
• Etsy.com	• Watchshopping.com
• EZTV	• Wikipedia
• Euro Pacific	• WordPress.com
• Expedia.com	• Zynga.com
• ExpressVPN.com	• Newegg.com
• Fancy.com	• Burger King
• Grooveshark	• Lieferando
• Gyft	• Subways
• Intuit	• Cheapair.com
• Lumfiles	• Royal Bank of Canada
• Mega.co.nz	• Bankera
• Microsoft	• University of Columbia
• Mint.com	• Intuit
• Namecheap.com	• REEDS Jewelers[xix]

How do you buy Bitcoin?

Bitcoin can primarily be purchased through exchanges and held, subsequently, in the exchange or in a wallet. Once an account is created on an exchange, users may transfer fiat currency into the account to purchase desired cryptocurrencies. Popular exchanges are listed here:

US

Coinbase - coinbase.com (best for new investors)

Binance US - binance.us (best for altcoins, advanced investors)

Bisq - bisq.network (decentralized)

Global (not available/limited functionality in the US)

Binance - binance.com (best overall)

Huibo Global -huobi.com (most offerings)

Crypto.com - crypto.com (lowest fees)

Is Bitcoin a good investment?

In historical terms, Bitcoin is one of the best investments of the past decade; the compounded rate of return has been about 200% a year and $10 put into Bitcoin in 2010 would be worth $7.6 million today (an astounding 76,500,000% return on investment). However, the rapid returns generated by Bitcoin in the past cannot sustain themselves indefinitely, and the question of whether Bitcoin *will be* a good investment is another one entirely. Generally, the facts currently make Bitcoin out to be a good long-term hold, especially if you believe in the accelerating trends of decentralization and blockchain. That said, any number of black swan events could do extreme damage to Bitcoin, and any number of competitors could overtake Bitcoin's spot. The question of whether to invest should be backed up by facts and based on you: the amount of risk you're willing to take on, the amount of money you're able and willing to risk, and so on. So, do your research, think as rationally as possible, and make trading decisions you won't regret.

Will Bitcoin crash?

Bitcoin is a very cyclical asset and tends to regularly crash. For long-term Bitcoin holders, flash crashes and sustained bear periods are overwhelmingly likely. Bitcoin has crashed 80% or more (a number considered disastrous in other markets) three different times since 2012; in all occurrences, it has rapidly bounced back. All of this is partly because Bitcoin is still in its price discovery phase and growing rapidly in terms of adoption. So, while Bitcoin undoubtedly will crash, it will also undoubtedly (historically speaking) recover.

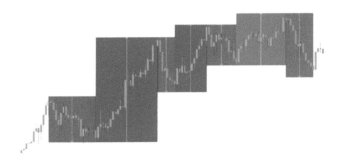

The above chart displays the up and down periods of Bitcoin in 2021; the mean average loss is 25.94%, while the mean average gain is 58.36%. Data and core image assets from coindesk.com.

What is Bitcoin's PoW system?

A PoW algorithm is used to confirm transactions and create new blocks on a given blockchain. PoW, meaning proof of work, literally means that work (through mathematical equations) is required to create blocks. The people who do the work are miners, and miners are rewarded for their computational effort through equity.

Miners use computational power to find a hash value by solving a complex mathematical equation

↓

When a hash value is found, the discovery is announced to the network, and a new block is created.

↓

The miner who solved the equation and found the hash value receives a reward of the mined coin.

What is Bitcoin halving?

Halving is a supply mechanism that governs the rate at which coins are added to a fixed-supply cryptocurrency. The idea and process were popularized by Bitcoin, which halves every 4 years. Halving is set in motion by a programmed reduction in mining rewards; block rewards are the rewards given to the miners (really, the computers) that process and validate transactions in a given blockchain network. From 2016 to 2020, all the computers (called the nodes) in the Bitcoin network collectively earned 12.5 Bitcoin every 10 minutes, and that was the number of Bitcoins entering circulation. However, following May 11th, 2020, the rewards dropped to 6.25 Bitcoin per the same timeframe. In this way, for every 210,000 blocks mined, which equates to roughly every four years, the block rewards will continue to halve until the max limit of 21 million coins is reached around the year 2140. Thus, halving is likely to increase the value of Bitcoin and other cryptocurrencies by decreasing supply while not altering demand. Scarcity, as mentioned, drives value, and limited supply combined with growing demand creates greater and greater scarcity. For this reason, halving has historically driven the price of Bitcoin up and will likely remain a long-term growth catalyst.

The common historical cycle of Bitcoin in regard to halving is typically, a rapid run up period followed by a sharp correction, a period of sideways stability (accumulation) and a build-up to another rapid bull period. The below visual displays the price action of Bitcoin after halving events; three of such events are plotted, and the line represents the day of halving.

Why is Bitcoin volatile?

Bitcoin is still in its "price discovery phase" meaning the market is growing so fast that Bitcoin's true value remains unknown. Therefore, perceived value runs the market (furthered by the lack of any centralized control to manage Bitcoin volatility) and perceived value is very easily affected by news, rumors, and so on. Eventually, Bitcoin will become less volatile, but it could certainly take a while.

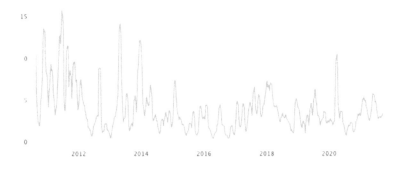

The above graph displays the standard deviation of Bitcoin daily returns (and therefore of Bitcoin volatility) from 2012 to 2021. For a means of comparison, the volatility of gold is around 1%, while most fiat currencies hang around 0.5% and 1.0%. Bitcoin, on the other hand, has gotten as high as 15% and averages 4.0%. Data and image assets from buybitcoinworldwide.com

Should I invest in Bitcoin?

The question of whether you should invest in Bitcoin is not only a matter of Bitcoin, but of you. Bitcoin carries an inherent risk, being a speculative and volatile asset, and while the potential upside is massive, the double-edged sword of risk and reward must be kept in mind. The best thing you can do is to learn as much as possible about Bitcoin, cryptocurrencies, and blockchain (as well as trends in such subjects and real-world developments), and mesh that information into your risk tolerance, financial situation, and whatever other variables may affect your investment decision. Therefore, in response to this question, the entire book should serve as a collective answer.

How do I successfully invest in Bitcoin?

These 5 rules will help you successfully invest in Bitcoin, being that money and trading are emotional experiences:

- ❖ Nothing lasts forever
- ❖ No woulda, shoulda, coulda
- ❖ Don't be emotional
- ❖ Diversify
- ❖ Prices don't matter

Nothing Lasts Forever

Historically, Bitcoin has operated through cycles that involve massive bull runs, the largest of which occurred in late 2017, March to July of 2019, and again from November of 2020 to early April 2021. In the mentioned bull runs, respectively, Bitcoin went up roughly 15x (2017), 3x (2019), and 10x+. In the one previous case in which Bitcoin went up more than 15x, the better part of the following year was then spent crashing from 20k to 4k. This supports the idea of the mentioned Bitcoin cycles, which first have a massive uptrend, and then crash to higher lows. This conclusion supports several strategies: one, it is a good bet to hold if

Bitcoin is crashing. Two, if Bitcoin and the crypto market is going up while you're reading this, it will probably go down at some point in the next few years. If it is going down while you're reading this, it will likely go up in a truly massive way in the next few years. Of course, the market ecosystem is liable to change, but this is the exact point to be made. Assuming that cryptocurrencies reach mass adoption and become an integral part of all aspects of money, business, and general life, *it will have to stabilize* at some point. That point may be in 2021, 2023, or 2030. It will likely crash and rise multiple times before steadying into a somewhat less volatile market, at least relative to its former self.

No Woulda, Shoulda, Coulda

This rule is taken from a popular and legendary stock trader and host of the show *Mad Money*, Jim Cramer. This concept works across all investments, not to mention across all walks of life, and ties into rule #3. The idea is represented through no woulda, no shoulda, and no coulda. This means that if you make a bad trade, take a few minutes to think about how you can learn from it and improve; then, after those few minutes, don't think about what you *would* have done, what you *should* have done, or what you *could* have done. This will allow you to learn and improve while simultaneously maintaining sanity, because, at the end of the day, you always could have done it better. Don't beat yourself up about losses and don't let wins get to your head.

Don't Be Emotional

Emotion is the antithesis of technical trading. Technical trading bases current and future action on historical data and, sadly, the market doesn't care how you feel. Emotion, more often than not ("not" simply due to the random occurrence of making a good decision through a bad process) will only hurt you and take away from the trading strategies you have developed. Some people are naturally comfortable with the risk and emotional rollercoaster of trading; if you're not, you should consider learning about the psychology of trading (because understanding emotions is a predecessor to acceptance, rationality, and control) and by simply giving yourself time. Fundamental analysis and mid-to-long-term trading still require all of this, but to a lesser degree.

Diversify

Diversification counters risk. And, as we know, crypto is risky. While anyone investing in cryptocurrencies both assumes and likely looks for a certain level of risk (due to the risk-return tradeoff principle), you do (probably) have a certain level of risk that you're not comfortable with. Diversification helps you stay within that maximum load of risk. While I can't speak to your unique situation, I would recommend to any crypto investor to maintain a somewhat diversified portfolio, no matter how much you believe in a project. Fund allocation should (usually) be split between Bitcoin, Etherium or ETH alternatives (such as Cardano, BNB, etc) and various altcoins, along with some cash. While exact percentages vary depending on individual situation (35/25/30/10, 60/25/10/5, 20/20/40/20, etc), most professionals would agree that this is the most sustainable way to invest, capture gains across the market, and lower the chances of losing a large percentage of your portfolio due to one or a few mistaken decisions. However, all that said, some investors only put money into one or two top-50 cryptos and put most of their money into small-cap altcoins. At the end of the day, establish a strategy that fits your situation, resources, and personality, and then diversify within the boundaries of that strategy.

Price Doesn't Matter

Price is largely irrelevant since supply and initial price can both be set. Just because Binance Coin (BNB) is at $500 and Ripple (XRP) is at $1.80 doesn't mean that XRP is worth 277x BNB; in fact, the two coins are currently within 10% of each other's market cap. When a cryptocurrency is first created, the supply is set by the team behind the asset; the team may choose to create 1 trillion coins, or 10 million. So, looking back at XRP and BNB, we can see that Ripple has roughly 45 billion coins in circulation and Binance Coin has 150 million. In this way, price doesn't really matter. A coin at $0.0003 can be worth more than a coin at $10,000 in terms of market cap, circulating supply, volume, users, utility, etc. Price matters even less due to fractional shares, which lets investors invest any amount of money in a coin or token regardless of price. Many other metrics are much more important and should be considered well before price. That said, prices can affect price action as a result of psychology. For example: Bitcoin has strong resistance at $50,000 and much of this resistance may come from the fact that $50,000 is a nice, round number that many people would place buy orders and sell orders at. Through situations such as this and others, psychology is a viable part of price action and, hence, analysis.

Conclusions:

Nothing lasts forever. Trade as such.

↓

No woulda, shoulda, coulda. Keep your sanity.

↓

Don't be emotional. Pursue objective decision-making.

↓

Diversify. Crypto is risky enough.

↓

Price does not matter as much as utility, volume, and other metrics.

Does Bitcoin have intrinsic value?

No, Bitcoin does not have intrinsic value. Nothing about Bitcoin demands that it has value; rather, value is user-generated. However, by such a definition, all currencies of the world not backed by a gold or silver standard also have no intrinsic value (other than material use, which is insignificant). So, in a sense, all money only has any degree of value because we agree it does, and any arguments against or for the use of Bitcoin because of its lack of intrinsic value must also be applied to fiat currencies.

Traits of Money	Bitcoin	Gold	Fiat
Verifiable	High	Moderate	Moderate
Fungible	High	High	High
Portable	High	Low	High
Durable	Moderate	High	Low
Divisible	High	Low	Moderate
Scarce	High	Moderate	Low
Established History	Low	High	Low
Censorship resistant	High	Moderate	Low
Unforgeable Costliness	High	High	Low
*Openly Programmable	High	Low	Low
*Decentralized	High	Moderate	Low

Does Bitcoin get taxed?

As the saying goes, we can't avoid taxes, and such an idea certainly applies to cryptocurrency despite the seemingly anonymous and unregulated nature of the industry. For the most accurate information, you should visit the website of your tax-collection organization to learn more about digital currency tax in your country. That said, the following information places a spotlight on US-set rules:

• In 2014, the IRS declared that virtual currencies are property, not currency.

• If cryptocurrencies are received as payment for goods or services, the fair market value (in USD) must be taxed as income.

• If a coin or token is held for more than a year and it's sold at a gain, it's classified as a long-term gain, and if it is bought and sold within a year, it's a short-term gain. Short-term gains are subject to higher taxes than long-term gains.

• Income from mining virtual currencies is regarded as self-employment income (assuming the given individual is not an employee) and is subject to self-employment tax as per the fair equivalent value of the digital currencies in USD. Up to $3,000 of losses may be recognized.

- When digital currencies are sold, profits or losses are subject to capital gains tax (since the digital currencies are regarded as property) just as if a stock was sold.

Does Bitcoin trade 24/7?

Bitcoin does operate 24/7. This, in large part, is because Bitcoin is meant to be used all around the world, as a truly intercontinental tool, and given time zones, anything but 24/7 operation wouldn't meet those criteria. There also just isn't any incentive not to do so.

Does Bitcoin use fossil fuels?

Yes, Bitcoin uses fossil fields. In fact, many fossil-fuel power plants have found new life in providing the power needed to mine cryptocurrencies. Bitcoin uses about as much power as a small country purely through computational requirements, equivalent to about 0.55% of global electricity production. Obviously, Bitcoin users and miners don't want to use fossil fuels and a transition to renewable energy sources is a major goal, but the same could be said about driving gas-powered cars and the multitude of other daily activities that consume much more fossil fuel than Bitcoin. The problem really comes down to opinion; those who see Bitcoin as a pioneering force in the world that assists people in unstable financial ecosystems and enables greater security and privacy in transactions won't be concerned by a 0.55% global energy usage (especially given the promise of a long-term transition to clean energy), while those who view Bitcoin as worthless or a scam are likely to feel exactly the opposite. It should be noted that some cryptocurrency alternatives are much less carbon-intensive than Bitcoin (Cardano, ADA), carbon-neutral (Bitgreen, BITG), or carbon-negative (eGold, EGLD).

Will Bitcoin hit 100k?

Bitcoin is likely to hit $100,000 per coin. This doesn't mean that it will happen soon, or that it's a sure thing; just that data on the deflationary nature of Bitcoin, historical returns, adoption trends (if you're interested, research the "S" curve in technology), and fiat inflation renders a price increase to $100,000 as probable. The important question is not if it will hit $100,000, but when it will hit $100,000. Most of such estimates are, at best, educated speculation.

Will Bitcoin hit 1 million?

Unlike $100,000, Bitcoin hitting $1 million requires some serious scale. A notable figure in finance has said that Bitcoin won't fulfill its potential until it's worth $1 million per coin, because at such a time each Satoshi (which is the smallest division Bitcoin can be split into) would be worth $1 cent. Given economies of scale and the potential for worldwide mass adoption (in such a case, Bitcoin would act as a universal reserve currency), it is possible that the price could hit $1 million. However, another cryptocurrency could just as easily take this spot, as well as government-backed stablecoins or digital currencies. In combination, it should be noted that fiat currencies are inflationary, and Bitcoin is deflationary. This price dynamic renders $1 million much more likely in the long-term. Ultimately, however, it's anyone's guess what could happen, and a $1 million per coin valuation remains speculative.

1M ⊙

PEAK PRICE

Will Bitcoin keep going up this fast?

No. It is quite literally impossible. Bitcoin has returned investors 200% per year for the past 10 years, which works out to a 5.2 million percent return over the decade. Given the market cap of Bitcoin at the time of this writing, a sustained compounded increase of 200% would overrun the entire monetary supply of the world in less than a decade. So, while it is entirely possible that Bitcoin will keep going up, growth must flatten in the long-term and volatility is likely to decrease. In the below visual, the effects of a 2020-repeat bull run are shown; such a run would incur a ten-trillion-dollar valuation. While this is possible at some point in the future, such a run-up and others like it must cease in scale at some point.

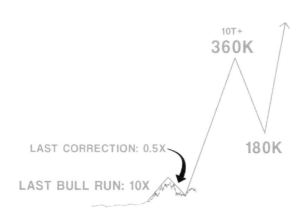

What are Bitcoin forks?

A fork is the occurrence of a new blockchain being created from another blockchain. Bitcoin has had 105 forks, the largest of which is the present-day Bitcoin Cash. Forks occur when an algorithm is split into two different versions. Two primary types of forks exist: hard forks, which occur when all the nodes in the network upgrade to a newer version of the blockchain and leave the old version behind (two paths are then created: the new version and the old version), and a soft fork, which contrasts this by rendering the old network invalid (resulting in just one blockchain)

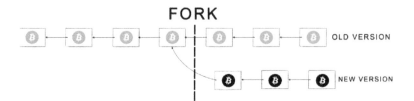

Why does Bitcoin fluctuate?

As with the stock market, price rises and falls as per demand and supply. Demand and supply, in turn, are affected by the cost of producing a bitcoin on the blockchain, news, competitors, internal governance, and whales (large holders). For information on why Bitcoin is as volatile as it is, please refer to the multitude of other questions on the subject. As displayed in the following visuals, the inelastic supply of Bitcoin makes prices more responsive to small changes in demand. Image source: Matias Antonio (hackernoon.com).

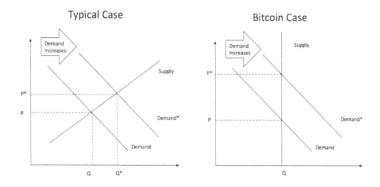

How do Bitcoin wallets work?

A crypto wallet is the interface used to manage crypto holdings; Coinbase wallet and Exodus are the most common of such wallets. An account, in turn, is a pair of public and private keys from which you can control your funds, which are stored on the blockchain. Simply put, wallets are accounts that store your holdings for you, just like a bank.

xxii

*Wallets do not contain coins. Wallets contain pairs of private and public keys, which provide access to holdings.

Does Bitcoin work in all countries?

Bitcoin is a decentralized network of computers; all addresses are unblockable and therefore accessible anywhere with a web connection. In countries where Bitcoin is illegal (the largest of which are China and Russia), all the government can do is crack down on the infrastructure (specifically mining farms) and usage of Bitcoin. In places such as Russia, Bitcoin is not actually regulated, rather, the use of Bitcoin as payment for goods and services is illegal. Most other countries follow this model, since again, blocking Bitcoin itself is impossible. In fact, the SEC's Hester Peirce has stated that "governments would be foolish to ban Bitcoin." Given this, it may be said that Bitcoin works in all countries, though in some you are simply not allowed to use it. The image on the next page provides information on the legality of Bitcoin throughout the world.

Legality of Bitcoin throughout the world:

| Legal tender
| Permissive (it's legal to use bitcoin)
| Contentious (some restrictions on legal usage of bitcoin)
| Contentious (interpretation of old laws, but bitcoin isn't prohibited directly)
| Hostile (full or partial prohibition)
| No information.

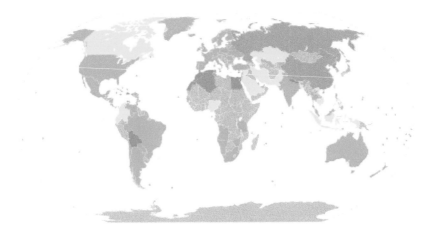

*This information is extremely liable to change. China appears to have since banned the use of Bitcoin, and information on other countries, again, is not confirmed to be correct. Please confirm the use of cryptocurrencies is legal in your country before use.

How many people have Bitcoin?

The best estimation[6] currently places the number at about 100 million global holders, which accounts for roughly 1 in every 55 adults. That said, the true number is unknowable given the anonymous nature of crypto networks. It can be said that user growth is in the high double-digits, Bitcoin has several hundred thousand transactions per day, 2+ billion people have heard of Bitcoin, and about half a billion Bitcoin addresses exist in total. The following visual (data from statistica.com) displays the number of identity-verified cryptocurrency users over time.

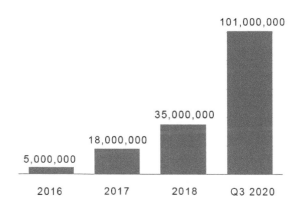

Who has the most Bitcoin?

The mysterious founder of Bitcoin, Satoshi Nakamoto, owns the most Bitcoin. He holds 1.1 million BTCs across multiple wallets, giving him a net worth in the tens of billions. If Bitcoin hit $180,000, Satoshi Nakamoto would become the richest person on Earth. Following Satoshi Nakamoto, the Winklevoss twins and various law enforcement agencies are the largest holders (the FBI became one of the largest Bitcoin holders after seizing the assets of the Silk Road, an internet black market that was shut down in 2013).

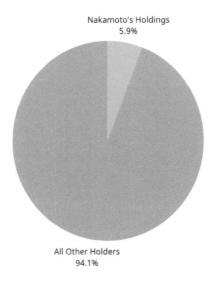

Nakamoto's Holdings
5.9%

All Other Holders
94.1%

*Based off the current circulating supply, not the maximum supply.

Can you trade Bitcoin with algorithms?

To answer this question, I'll include an excerpt from another one of my books about Cryptocurrency Technical Analysis. The following covers all bases and occupies a few pages, so if you're looking for a short answer, I'll say that you can, but it's difficult.

Algorithmic trading is the art of getting a computer to make money for you. Or, at least, that's the goal. Algo traders, as the slang goes, attempt to identify a set of rules that, if used as a foundation to trade upon, turn a profit. When these rules are chosen and triggered, code will execute an order. For example: say you love trading with exponential moving average crossovers (EMA's). Whenever you see Bitcoin's 12-day EMA pass the 50-day EMA, you invest 0.01 bitcoin. Then, you typically sell when you've made a 5% profit or, if it isn't working out, you cut your losses at 5%. It would be very easy to convert this preferred trading strategy into algorithmic trading rules. You'd code an algorithm that would track all the data of Bitcoin, invest your 0.01 bitcoin during your preferred EMA crossover, and then sell at either a 5% profit or a 5% loss. This algorithm would run for you while you sleep, while you eat, literally 24/7 or during a time you set. Since it only trades exactly as you set it; you're very comfortable with the risk. Even if the algorithm works just 51 out of every 100 trades, you technically are turning a profit and could simply continue forever without putting in any work. Or you could consult more data and improve your algorithm to work 55/100 times, or 70/100. Ten years later, you're now a multi-trillionaire making money every second of every day while you sip tropical juice on a sunny beach.

5%	5%	5%	5%	5%	5%	5%	5%	5%	5%	5%	5%	5%	5%	5%	5%	5%	5%	5%	5%
5%	5%	5%	5%	5%	5%	5%	5%	5%	5%	5%	5%	5%	5%	5%	5%	5%	5%	5%	5%
5%	5%	5%	5%	5%	5%	5%	5%	5%	5%	5%	5%	5%	5%	5%	5%	5%	5%	5%	5%
5%	5%	5%	5%	5%	5%	5%	5%	5%	5%	5%	5%	5%	5%	5%	5%	5%	5%	5%	5%
5%	5%	5%	5%	5%	5%	5%	5%	5%	5%	5%	5%	5%	5%	5%	5%	5%	5%	5%	5%
5%	5%	5%	5%	5%	5%	5%	5%	5%	5%	5%	5%	5%	5%	5%	5%	5%	5%	5%	5%
5%	5%	5%	5%	5%	5%	5%	5%	5%	5%	5%	5%	5%	5%	5%	5%	5%	5%	5%	5%
5%	5%	5%	5%	5%	5%	5%	5%	5%	5%	5%	5%	5%	5%	5%	5%	5%	5%	5%	5%
5%	5%	5%	5%	5%	5%	5%	5%	5%	5%	5%	5%	5%	5%	5%	5%	5%	5%	5%	5%
5%	5%	5%	5%	5%	5%	5%	5%	5%	5%	5%	5%	5%	5%	5%	5%	5%	5%	5%	5%

Sadly, it is not that easy, but that is the concept of algorithmic trading. The nice hypothetical aspect of trading with a machine is that the income ceiling is practically limitless (or, at the very least, immensely scalable). Consider the above chart. This is a visualization of an algorithm that trades 200 times per day if certain conditions are met. The algorithm will exit the position either at a 5% profit or a 5% loss, as in the above example. Let's assume that you give the algorithm $10,000 to work with and 100% of the portfolio is put into each trade. Red signifies an unprofitable trade (a 5% loss) and green signifies a good trade, a 5% gain.

As per the chart, this algorithm is correct just 51% of the time. At this minute majority, a $10,000 investment would become $11,025 in just one day, $186,791.86 in 30 days, and, after one full year of trading, the result would be $29,389,237,672,608,055,000. That's 29 quintillion dollars, which is roughly 783 times as much as the total value of every single US dollar in circulation. Obviously, that wouldn't work. However, let's now assume that the algorithm, given the same rules, makes a profitable trade just 50.1% of the time, which means 1 extra profitable trade out of every 1,000. After 1 year, this algorithm would turn $10,000 into $14,400, then after 10 years, just under $400,000, and after 50 years, $835,437,561,881.32. That's 835 billion dollars (check it out for yourself with Moneychimp's compound interest calculator).

This seems easy. Just use historical data to test algorithms until you've found one that's at least 50.1% profitable, get $10k, and your kids will be trillionaires. Sadly, this doesn't work, and here are some of the challenges facing algorithmic traders:

Errors

The most obvious challenge is that of creating an error-free algorithm. Many services today make the process much easier and don't require as much coding experience, but some still require some level of coding ability and the rest a degree of technical knowledge. As I'm sure you can imagine, any misstep in creating an algorithm can result in game over. That's why you probably shouldn't code it yourself, unless you actually know how to code, in which case you should probably still consult a friend!

Unpredictable data

Just as with technical analysis as a whole, the expectation that historical patterns are likely to repeat is the foundation on which algorithmic trading rests. Black Swan events* and unpredictable factors, such as news, global crisis, quarterly reports, and so on, all can throw an algorithm off and render a previous strategy unprofitable.

Lack of adaptability

The challenge of unpredictable data is coupled with an inability to adapt to circumstances given new, contextual data. In this way, manual updates may be required. The solution to this problem is obviously AI that learns, improves, and tests, but this is far from reality and, if it worked, probably wouldn't be all that good for the market, since a few influential players could simply monetize it for their own use (given that it would be a literal money-printing machine) or share it with everyone, in which case the self-destruction challenge (below) applies.

Slippage, volatility, and flash crashes

Since algorithms play by set rules, they can be "tricked" through volatility and rendered unprofitable through slippage. For example, a small altcoin may jump several percent, whether up or down, in seconds. An algorithm might see the price hit the limit sell order and trigger liquidation, despite the price simply jumping back up to the previous price or higher.

Self-destruction

In the hypothetical occurrence of an intelligent AI that sorts through all available data, identifies the best possible trading algorithms, puts them into practice, and adapts to circumstances, multiple such AIs would eradicate their own trading strategies. For example: say 1 million of these AI's exist (really, many more people than this would use it if it became available for purchase). All the AIs would immediately discover the best algorithm and start trading on it. If this happened, the resulting influx of volume would render the strategy useless. The same scenario does occur today, except without the AI. Really good trading strategies are likely to be discovered by multiple people, then used and shared until they no longer are profitable or as profitable as they once were. In this way, good strategies and algorithms impede their own progress.

So, those are the challenges that prevent algorithmic trading from being a perfect, 4-hour workweek, tropical vacation-inducing, money-printing machine. That said, algorithms can certainly still be profitable. Many large firms and companies base their business solely on profitable trading algorithms. So, while trading bots shouldn't be thought of as easy money, they should be regarded as a discipline that can be mastered if enough time and effort is provided. Here are some highlights of algorithmic trading and how you can get started:

Backtesting

Since algorithms take a certain input and react accordingly, algo traders can backtest their algorithms against historical data. For example, going with the previous examples, if Trader X wants to make an algorithm that trades upon EMA crossovers, Trader X could test the algorithm by running it through every single year that the entire market has been in existence. The returns would then be plotted, and through split-testing Trader X can come up with a formula that has been historically proven to work without ever actually having put money on the table. In this way, you can test your own algorithms and play around with different variables to see how they affect overall returns.

Risk control

Backtesting is a great way to mitigate risk. The best alternative is through the disciplined and researched use of stop losses and trailing stop-losses. Both tools are elaborated upon in the risk management section.

Simplicity

Many people have concepts of algorithm trading that necessitate complex, multi-layered, code that involves multiple, if not a dozen or more, indicators, patterns, or oscillators. While unknowns cannot be accounted for, most successful algorithms used by professionals and non-professionals alike are surprisingly un-complex. Most involve one indicator, or perhaps the combination of two. I suggest you follow this established route if you're getting into algorithmic trading, but that said, if you do discover an extremely complex and superior algorithm, I will be the first to sign up!

*The prior text is an excerpt from the book Crypto Technical Analysis, also by the authors.

How will Bitcoin affect the future?

Bitcoin was the first successful large-scale use case for blockchain; the question of how blockchain will affect the future is a much larger question than that of Bitcoin's sole potential impact, much of which has previously been covered. Here are fields in which blockchain (and by extension, Bitcoin) will have or is having a major effect:

- Supply chain management
- Logistics management
- Secure data management
- Cross-border payments and means of transaction
- Artist royalty tracking
- Secure storing and sharing of medical data
- NFT marketplaces
- Voting mechanisms and security
- Verifiable ownership of real estate
- Real estate marketplace
- Invoice reconciliation and dispute resolution
- Ticketing
- Financial guarantees
- Disaster recovery efforts
- Connecting suppliers and distributor
- Origin tracing

- Proxy voting
- Cryptocurrency
- Proof of insurance / insurance policies
- Health / personal data records
- Capital access
- Decentralized finance
- Digital identity
- Process / logistical efficiency
- Data verification
- Claims processing (insurance)
- IP protection
- Digitization of assets and financial instruments
- Governmental financial corruption reduction
- Online gaming
- Syndicated loans
- And more!

Is Bitcoin the future of money?

The question of whether Bitcoin itself is the "future of money" is speculation; the real question is whether the technology behind Bitcoin and the systems that Bitcoin encourages are the future of money. If so, investing in cryptocurrency, as well as Bitcoin (although growth potential in % in Bitcoin is limited relative to smaller coins given the volume of money already in it) is a very good bet.

The major technology fueling Bitcoin is blockchain, and the overall system Bitcoin encourages is that of decentralization. Both fields are exploding across a multitude of expanding use cases, and each has the potential to affect every aspect of life, from payments to work to voting. To quote Capgemini Engineering, "it [blockchain] improves safety and security significantly in the finance, healthcare, supply chain, software, and government sectors." Companies using blockchain technology includes Amazon (through AWS), BMW (in logistics), Citigroup (in finance), Facebook (through the creation of its own cryptocurrency), General Electric (supply chain), Google (with BigQuery), IBM, JPMorgan, Microsoft, Mastercard, Nasdaq, Nestlé, Samsung, Square, TenCent, T-Mobile, the United Nations, Vanguard, Walmart, and more.[7] The expanded clientele and products powered by or centered around blockchain signal the progression of blockchain into a core aspect of internet and offline services. With all this in mind, Bitcoin isn't limited to having an impact within cryptocurrencies, rather, it can and likely will usher in an era of blockchain. In terms of Bitcoin being the future of money and payments, the important question is how governments respond to Bitcoin and cryptocurrencies. Some, like China, may develop their own digital currencies. Some, like El Salvador, may make Bitcoin legal tender. Others yet may ignore cryptocurrencies or ban them all together. In whatever way governments react, the fact that they will be forced to react means that Bitcoin was the flagship that, in one way or another, will completely alter the financial landscape of the world through the successful application of digital and blockchain-driven assets.

BITCOIN   BLOCKCHAIN

How many people are Bitcoin billionaires?

It's tough to know how many billionaires exist in the crypto space or even just within the crypto network since holdings are often split up over multiple accounts. However, excluding the holdings of exchanges, twenty Bitcoin addresses hold the equivalent of $1 billion or more, and eighty Bitcoin addresses hold the equivalent of $500 million or more.[xxiii] This number can easily fluctuate, since many of the wallets worth $500 million to $1 billion can rise past $1 billion in alignment with Bitcoin fluctuation, and as mentioned, holders who sold Bitcoin or split their holdings among multiple wallets are not included. That said, it's safe to say that at least two dozen accounts, and at least 1 dozen people, have made more than $1 billion dollars by investing in Bitcoin. Dozens more have made hundreds of millions or billions by investing in other cryptocurrencies.

Fun fact: the number of bitcoins required to make a billionaire is currently 22,727; this is less than a quarter of the amount that the infamous Laszlo Hanyecz collected and spent in the early days of Bitcoin. If he'd held, he would currently have a net worth of 3.8 billion. He didn't, unfortunately, and you may know him as the man who spent 10,000 bitcoin on a pizza. Still, he claims he has no regrets.

$1 MILLION = 23 BITCOIN

$1 BILLION = 22,727 BITCOIN

Are there secret Bitcoin billionaires?

Satoshi Nakamoto is the prime example of a secret and anonymous Bitcoin billionaire. In the question above (How many people are Bitcoin billionaires?), we arrived at the conclusion that at least 1 dozen people have made a billion dollars by investing in Bitcoin. Given this number, and the fact that the number of popular Bitcoin billionaires can be counted on one hand (individual people, not including corporations), it is presumable that a few Bitcoin holders around the world are Bitcoin billionaires who have stayed out of the limelight. With that thought in mind, you may, at some point, have been going about your day and crossed paths with a secret Bitcoin billionaire.

Will Bitcoin reach mainstream adoption?

This is an interesting question. Currently, around 1% of the world uses Bitcoin, although this deviates all the way to 20% in places like America, and down to 0% in other parts of the world. For a cryptocurrency to reach mainstream and mass adoption, it must serve some sort of utility. Generally, cryptocurrencies have utility as a store of value; a method of transacting, or as a framework to build networks and decentralized organizations. Bitcoin is by far the largest and the most valuable cryptocurrency, but it isn't the best cryptocurrency in any of those categories. So, while Bitcoin is Bitcoin (much like how you could buy a cheaper watch than a Rolex that fits better and looks nicer, but you still go with Rolex) and the brand of Bitcoin has and will go far, it is unlikely to be the permanent leader among cryptocurrencies in the world. That said, given its brand equity and scale, it may almost certainly reach mass and mainstream adoption, given current usage trends and an expanding clientele of use cases in the cryptocurrency space.

Will Bitcoin get taken over by other cryptocurrencies?

I'll refer to the above question in answering this. Bitcoin, while massive in scale and brand, isn't the best at anything in the crypto space. It's not the best store of value, it's not the best for sending and receiving money, and it's not the best as a framework and network for crypto users to operate and build upon. So, in the short term, given the pure brand of Bitcoin and its monstrous $1 trillion market cap, it is unlikely to get taken over. However, within decades or centuries, it is more than likely to get passed by other cryptocurrencies as the value that fuels it disintegrates.

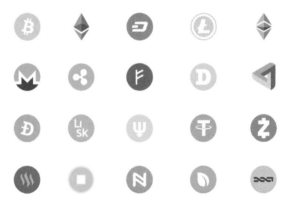

Can Bitcoin change from PoW?

Yes, Bitcoin can certainly change from a PoW (proof-of-work) system. Ethereum started out on PoW and is expected to switch to PoS (proof-of-stake) in late 2021. The switch will render Ethereum much less energy-intensive and more scalable. A transition like this is certainly possible for Bitcoin and many consider a move away from PoW inevitable. The following visual displays the relative energy consumption per transaction of Bitcoin versus Ethereum following a transition to proof-of-stake; such a comparison is representative of the benefits a switch away from PoW can incur.

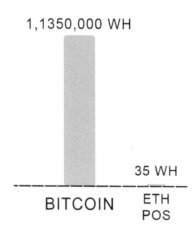

1,1350,000 WH

35 WH

BITCOIN   ETH
POS

Was Bitcoin the first ever cryptocurrency?

Satoshi Nakamoto's infamous Bitcoin white paper was released in 2008, and Bitcoin itself was released in 2009. These events are known as being the first of their respective kind; this is only partly true.

In the late 1980's, a group of developers in the Netherlands attempted to link money to cards to prevent rampant cash thievery. Truck drivers used these cards instead of cash; this is perhaps the first example of electronic cash. Around the same time as the Netherland experiment, American cryptographer David Chaum conceptualized a transferable and private token-based currency. He developed a "blinding formula" to be used in encryption, and founded the company DigiCash, which went belly-up in 1988.

In the 1990s, multiple companies attempted to succeed where DigiCash hadn't; the most popular of which was Elon Musk's PayPal. PayPal introduced easy P2P payments online and incurred the creation of a company called E-gold (not to be confused with the much more recent cryptocurrency of Elrond eGold), which offered online credit in exchange for precious metals. E-gold was later shut down by the government. Additionally, in 1991, researchers Stuart Haber and W. Scoot Stornetta described blockchain technology. Several years later, in 1997, the Hashcash project used a proof-of-work algorithm to generate and distribute new coins, and many of their features ended up in the original Bitcoin protocol. One year later, developer Wei Dai (after whom the smallest denomination of Ether, a Wei, is named) introduced the idea of an "anonymous, distributed electronic cash system" called B-money. B-money was meant to provide a decentralized network through which users could send and receive currency; unfortunately, it never got off the ground. Shortly following the B-money whitepaper, Nick Szabo launched a project called Bit Gold, which operated on a full PoW (proof-of-work) system. Bit gold, in fact, is relatively similar to Bitcoin.

All of these projects and dozens more eventually led to Bitcoin; for this reason, it cannot be said that Bitcoin was the true first in many of the concepts and technologies that enable it. That said, Bitcoin is absolutely and undoubtedly the first large-scale success of all the technologies that enable it; every single company and project before Bitcoin had failed, but Bitcoin ascended beyond the rest and instigated a massive global shift towards the technologies and concepts it is built upon.

Can Bitcoin be more than an alternative to gold?

Bitcoin already is "more" than an alternative to gold; it powers and enables a global transactional network with much less friction than gold. Bitcoin is much more comparative to gold in the fact that both are thought of as stores of value and a means of transaction. Regarding this, Bitcoin will probably never be more than an alternative to gold, because the alternative within the crypto ecosystem is being a technology or platform like Ethereum, which allows users to leverage its programming language, called Solidity, to create dApps. Bitcoin just isn't meant to do anything like that, and while it certainly has more utility than gold, it is somewhat typecasted into the role of being a "digital gold."

What is the latency of Bitcoin, and is it important?

Latency is the delay between the time it takes to submit a transaction and the time it takes the network to recognize the transaction; basically, latency is the lag. Bitcoin's latency is very high by design (relative to the 5-10 seconds of broadcast TV) in order to produce one new block every ten minutes. Lowering the latency would essentially require less work to verify blocks, which goes against the ethos of PoW. For this reason, Bitcoin's latency shouldn't be lowered. That said, trading latency is an issue for exchanges and traders on exchanges (especially arbitrage traders); as HFT (high frequency trading) and algorithmic trading moves into the cryptocurrency market, latency will increase in importance (MCT data from blockchain.com).

MEDIAN CONFIRMATION TIME: 7 MIN

What are some Bitcoin conspiracy theories?

Bitcoin (and especially Satoshi Nakamoto) is a ripe environment for conspiracy theories; just for fun, we'll look at a few. Consider the following completely fictional and not to be taken seriously.

1. *Bitcoin was created by the NSA or another U.S intelligence agency.* This is probably the most prevalent Bitcoin conspiracy; it asserts that Bitcoin was created by the U.S government, and that it isn't as private as we think. Instead, the theory states that the NSA has backdoor access to the SHA-256 algorithm and uses such access to spy on users.

2. *Bitcoin is an AI.* This theory states that Bitcoin is an AI which uses its economic motive to incentivize users to grow its network. Some believe that a government agency created the AI.

3. *Bitcoin was created by four major Asian companies.* This theory is completely based on the fact that the "sa" in Samsung, the "toshi" from Toshiba, the "naka" from Nakamichi, and the "moto" from Motorola, in combination, form the name of Bitcoin's secret founder, Satoshi Nakamoto. Quite solid evidence for this one.

Why do most other coins often follow Bitcoin?

Bitcoin is essentially the reserve currency for cryptocurrencies and the equivalent of the Dow and S&P for the stock market. About 50% of value in the cryptocurrency market lies solely with Bitcoin, and Bitcoin is the most used and best-known cryptocurrency in the world. For these reasons, Bitcoin trading pairs are the most-used pairs to buy Altcoins with, which ties the value of all other cryptocurrencies to Bitcoin. Bitcoin going down results in less money being put into Altcoins, while Bitcoin going up results in more money being put into Altcoins. For these reasons, most (not all) coins often (not always) follow the general trends of Bitcoin. Consider the following the charts; all seven display the same week; the top is Bitcoin, and the other six are popular cryptocurrencies.

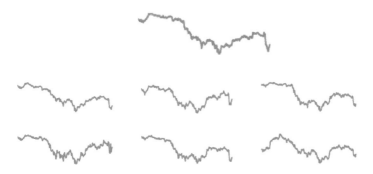

What is Bitcoin Cash?

As mentioned prior, Bitcoin has a scale problem; the network is simply not fast enough to handle the large amounts of transactions present in a global-adoption situation. Considering this, in 2017, a collective of Bitcoin miners and developers initiated a hard fork of Bitcoin. The new currency, called Bitcoin Cash (BCH), upped the block size (to 32MB in 2018), hence allowing the network to process more transactions than Bitcoin, and faster. While BCH isn't set to replace or come close to replacing Bitcoin (considering a current market cap of $10 billion), it is an alternative that solved a major problem, and the question of how the original Bitcoin will go about solving the same problem remains to be solved.

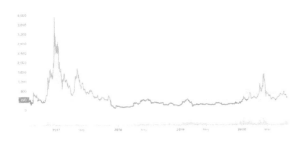

Bitcoin Cash price history, from 2017 to mid 2021 (*coinmarketcap.com*)[xxiv]

How will Bitcoin act during a recession?

Bitcoin has a great chance of performing well during a recession, though this is not a conclusive answer; Bitcoin arose out of the 2008 housing crisis but has yet to experience any sustained and major economic downturn since then (COVID doesn't count). In many ways, Bitcoin serves as a digital equivalent to gold, and gold has historically performed well during recessions (notably, from 2007 to 2012), and the scarcity and decentralized nature of Bitcoin could render it a safe-haven investment during a recession, one that wouldn't be subject to government control over fiat currencies and the inflationary monetary system of the world. It should also be noted that Bitcoin has historically risen during smaller-scale crises: Brexit, the Congress Crisis of 2013, and throughout the coronavirus epidemic. So, as previously asserted, Bitcoin will probably perform well during a recession. Either way, in the case of a recession, most cryptocurrencies other than Bitcoin (especially smaller altcoins) will undoubtably experience massive losses; most will practically be wiped off the map. Such a scenario would be a massive filter event for altcoins, which is very healthy scenario for the overall market and long-term adoption of cryptocurrencies.

Can Bitcoin survive in the long run?

What should be considered is to what extent Bitcoin will survive in the long run and to what degree adoption and usage will grow. Regardless, Bitcoin will exist to some scale for the next few decades and will exist as long as the internet remains around. That said, the chances of it lasting at scale for the next few centuries are improbable given newer competition and Bitcoin alternatives. Still, it certainly could remain the top cryptocurrency as long as cryptocurrencies are around (especially if upgrades, such as the lighting network, are implemented); the prior probability is based purely on the fact that the first of its kind isn't usually the best of its kind, and most currencies throughout history haven't lasted at scale for significant portion of time.

What is the end goal of Bitcoin and cryptos?

The end vision of cryptocurrency accomplishes the following:

1. For Bitcoin specifically: to give users the ability to transact value over the internet in a secure fashion without relying on a central institution, instead relying on cryptographic proof.

2. To eliminate the need of intermediaries and decrease friction in supply chains, banks, real estate, law, and other fields.

3. To eliminate the dangers faced by the inflationary, wild-west (in regard to government control since fiat currencies were taken off the gold standard) environment of fiat currencies.

4. To enable secure control over personal assets without relying on third-party institutions.

5. To enable blockchain solutions in medical, logistical, voting, and finance fields, in addition to wherever else such solutions may apply.

Is Bitcoin too expensive to use as a cryptocurrency?

Absolute price is largely irrelevant for cryptocurrencies (as well as for stocks, as I've written about in other books). While this answer has been covered elsewhere in the trading rules, I'll recap the relevant section below:

Given that supply and initial price can both be set/altered, price itself is largely irrelevant without context. Just because Binance Coin (BNB) is at $500 and Ripple (XRP) is at $1.80 doesn't mean that XRP is worth 277x the value of BNB; the two coins are currently within 10% of each other's market cap. When a cryptocurrency is first created, the supply is set by the team behind the asset. The team may choose to create 1 trillion coins, or 10 million. Looking back at XRP and BNB, we can see that Ripple has roughly 45 billion coins in circulation, and Binance Coin has 150 million. In this way, price doesn't really matter. A coin at $0.0003 can be worth more than a coin at $10,000 in terms of market cap, circulating supply, volume, users, utility, etc. Price matters even less due to the advent of fractional shares, which lets investors invest any amount of money in a coin or token regardless of price. The only major impact of price lies in the psychological impact, which should be examined while trading Bitcoin and altcoins. Consider the visual; note that price does not correlate with ranking, market cap, or supply. Data from coinmarketcap.com

Price	Market Cap	Circulating Supply
$42,983.38	$807,337,903,756	18,825,281 BTC
$2,964.30	$347,697,842,229	117,660,467 ETH
$2.31	$73,665,185,651	32,038,100,544 ADA
$1.00	$68,622,996,686	68,592,705,856 USDT
$358.28	$60,099,829,044	168,137,036 BNB
$0.9521	$44,531,168,458	46,717,640,571 XRP
$141.51	$42,154,008,953	297,281,474 SOL
$31.05	$30,666,318,384	987,579,315 DOT
$0.9998	$30,682,132,886	30,688,745,774 USDC
$0.2108	$27,699,549,455	131,419,507,714 DOGE

How popular is Bitcoin?

At least 1.3% of the world currently owns Bitcoin, which, factoring in the half-billion Bitcoin addresses in existence, makes it quite popular. This number includes 46 million Americans, which is 14% of the population and 21% of adults, while another study found that 5% of Europeans hold Bitcoin. More notably, however, is the exponential rate of increase. Less than one million Bitcoin wallets existed in 2014, representing a 75x increase since then, and a growth rate of 10x (1,000%) per year. Such trends show no sign of stopping and growth, if anything, is only picking up. So, summarized, Bitcoin is notably popular and likely to reach a tipping-point of mass adoption in the next few decades if current trends are maintained. [xxv]

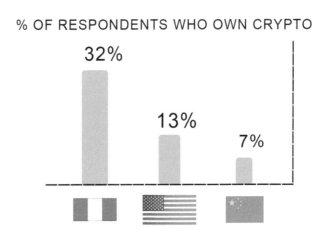

Resources

In the Resources Section:

- Essential Dictionary
- Books
- Exchanges
- Podcasts
- New Services
- Charting Services
- YouTube Channels

Crypto Essential Dictionary

A small dictionary (glossary, if you may) is included in this book to provide a solid foundation of knowledge (if needed), a source to refer to, and full comprehension of any topics previously discussed in this book. It is split into two sections: essential terms and trading terms. Essential terms are a few handpicked, important words that must be known in order to operate with confidence in the crypto space. It is brief, but worth spending a few minutes looking through. The second section, titled "crypto trading dictionary," consists of important terms related to technical analysis, all other forms of crypto analysis, and trading as a whole. It can be used if any words previously used in this book aren't understood or covered or to build a ground-up vocabulary. If any words were missed, not understood, or otherwise should be included, please contact me at the email at the end (or start) of this book, and I'll include your suggested edits in the next edition.

Account

An account is a pair of public and private keys (see below) from which you can control your funds. You typically view your account through an exchange, which provides an ideal trading interface (UI). However, your funds are actually stored on the blockchain, not in your account.

Address(es)

An address, also known as your public key, is a unique collection of numbers and letters that function as an identification code comparable to a bank account number or an email address. With it, you can carry out transactions on the blockchain. Addresses have round, colorful "logos" that are called address identicons (or, simply "icons"). These icons allow you to quickly see whether or not you input a correct address.

Airdrop

An airdrop is a marketing tool used by new coins. The team behind a new coin or token will give users the ability to receive the asset for free, typically in exchange for a small task, such as following the company on social media or providing your email address. Airdrops are great for the project since many new customers get excited about the coin and want to see it rise in value. It is also great for users since they get the coin for free and can potentially make a lot of money. However, airdrop scams are common, and many new coins fail, so make sure to do your research to understand which new airdrops are good and which airdrops aren't. Here are a few sites that provide information about new airdrops:

- airdrops.io
- airdropalert.com
- icomarks.com

Algorithm

An algorithm is the mathematical rules (the structure) that a code or software must follow. Many forms of algorithms are used across the internet, such as those used by social media services to decide which content gets how much exposure. Blockchains and cryptocurrencies use algorithms to perform a variety of tasks.

Altcoin(s)

Bitcoin was the first cryptocurrency, as well as the coin that popularized the industry. As a result, Bitcoin belongs to its own category, while all other coins are referred to as altcoins.

Bitcoin

Bitcoin was the first cryptocurrency. It was created in 2008 by an individual (or, more likely, a group of individuals) operating under the name Satoshi Nakamoto.

Cash

In the world of crypto and investments, cash does not mean keeping literal cash, but rather money that is not invested and is instead being held in an account as a digital balance.

Confirmed

This refers to a transaction being confirmed, which means multiple peers in the network have validated it. Once a transaction has been confirmed, it is permanently put in the public ledger.

dApp(s)/DAOs

dApp is short for "decentralized application." Basically, any app that runs on a blockchain (or any other peer-to-peer network) and does not have a centralized owner is considered a dApp. DAO is shorthand for decentralized autonomous organizations and refers to any organization run by a computer and not humans.

Decryption/Encryption

Encryption is the process of converting plain text into coded information through the use of a cipher. The opposite is decryption, which converts coded information into plain text.

Digital Commodity

A digital commodity is a digital asset that holds value. Digital commodities do not have to be digital currencies. They can be NFTs, digital art, or digital currencies.

Digital Currency

Digital currencies lie within the realm of digital commodities. Instead of referring to all digital assets, digital currencies refer to all currencies that operate only online and do not have a physical form.

Digital Signature

Your digital signature is used to confirm online documents. This isn't an actual signature; instead, it refers to a code generated by an algorithm.

Distributed Ledger

A distributed ledger is a ledger that is stored in many different locations so that multiple parties can validate transactions. Blockchain networks use distributed ledgers.

Dolphin/Whales

Crypto holders are classified through several different animals. Those with extremely large holdings, such as in the millions, are called whales, while those with moderately sized holdings are called dolphins.

Dump

To dump, or dumping, refers to selling a large amount of cryptocurrency or a large amount of a coin or token. For example, you might say, "that coin is dumping," or "I'm dumping this coin."

ERC-20/ERC-20 Standard

An ERC-20 is one of the many Ethereum tokens. Remember, a token is a token because it is built upon another blockchain. ERC-20 is significant in the world of Ethereum tokens because it is used to define the rules by which all tokens on the Ethereum blockchain function and creates a standardized structure. It can be likened to a security guard; it requires and ensures that all tokens in its vicinity follow that set of rules. The ERC-20 "standard" is the combined list of all the rules. Tokens using the ERC-20 standard can transact between each other and exchange in an easier and better manner.

Ether

Ether is the native cryptocurrency of the Ethereum blockchain. Its ticker symbol is ETH, and by using any currency on the Ethereum blockchain, you must pay the fees in Ether.

Exchange

A [crypto] exchange is a marketplace where cryptocurrencies and tokens can be bought, sold, and traded. Exchanges must be combined with wallets. In wallets, coins can be held through addresses. Exchanges act as an easy intermediary to help users interact with each other.

Fiat

Fiat refers to legal and centralized government currency, such as the US dollar or Euros.

Fintech

Fintech is short for financial technology. Fintech consists of any technology that supports and/or enables financial services. Cryptocurrencies are examples of fintech, as well as companies such as GoFundMe and PayPal.

Fork/Hard Fork/Soft Fork

A fork is the occurrence of a new blockchain being created from another blockchain. For example, Bitcoin Cash once forked off from Bitcoin. Forks (the process is actually much more complicated than this, but here is a simple overview) occur when algorithms have a disagreement and split into two different versions. Two kinds of forks exist: a hard fork and a soft fork. A hard fork in a blockchain is a fork that occurs when all the nodes in the network upgrade to a newer version of the blockchain and leave the old version behind. Two paths are then created: the new version and the old version. A soft fork contrasts this by rendering the old network invalid resulting in just one blockchain, not the two that emerge from a hard fork.

Fundamental Analysis

Fundamental analysis is the analysis of a coin or token through its underlying value. It aims to identify the "real value" (also known as the "fair market" value) of an asset through fundamental metrics, such as revenue, profit, cash flow, and an abundance of ratios.

Gas

Gas refers to the fee required to complete transactions on the Ethereum blockchain. Gas is basically the reward given to the miners that validate and complete the transaction.

Gwei

Gwei is the denomination (the price-per-unit) used in defining the cost of Ethereum gas (see above). You can think of Gwei and Ethereum as the dollar and the penny. 1 ETH equals one billion Gwei. Gwei is used instead of Ethereum because it is somewhat easier to say that gas fees are 1 Gwei than 0.0000000001 Ether.

Halving

Halving is the process by which the reward for mining Bitcoin is cut in half. Bitcoin halving happens every 210,000 blocks, which roughly equates to every 4 years. Halving will happen until the maximum supply (see below) of Bitcoin has been reached, and all 21 million coins have been put into circulation.

Hash/Hash Rate

A hash is a function that converts one value into another; a hash in the crypto world converts an input of letters and numbers (a string) into an encrypted output of a fixed size. Basically, hashes help with encryption. "Solving" each hash requires working backward to solve an extremely complex mathematical problem. The measure by which a computer is judged in terms of its ability to hash is called a hash rate. Put simply, the hash rate is the speed at which a node can perform hashing.

Hot Wallet/Cold Wallet

A hot wallet refers to a cryptocurrency wallet connected to the internet; the opposite, cold storage, refers to a wallet that is not connected to the internet. Hot wallets allow the account owner to send and receive tokens; however, cold storage is more secure than hot storage.

Initial Coin Offering (ICO)

To raise funds and awareness, the creators of a cryptocurrency will put an initial portion of their coins up for purchase.

Initial Exchange Offering (IEO)

IEO's are similar to ICO's (initial coin offerings) in the sense that both are initial offerings of coins or tokens used solely within the crypto space. IEO's are coming into fashion as the "next ICO's" because IEO's allow online crypto trading platforms to make the asset tradeable directly. Basically, IEO's require less effort to invest in and streamline the trading process of an initial offering.

Keys

A key is a random string of characters that are used by algorithms to encrypt data. Two keys are used for cryptocurrency: a public key and a private key. Both are important to understand and are defined below in depth.

Mining

Mining is the process by which blocks are added to a blockchain by solving a mathematical problem. Solving these problems takes an extremely large amount of computational power; hence, rewards are provided to those who do the work. People or organizations who use their computational power to mine are known as "miners."

Network

A network, at its core, is an interconnected system. The system within a cryptocurrency network is made up of many nodes that assist the blockchain in various tasks. Basically, a crypto network can be thought of as many different computers working together to run the blockchain.

Node

A node is a computer (a node can be any computer; there aren't any special types) connected to a blockchain's network and assists the blockchain in writing and validating blocks. Some nodes download an entire history of their blockchain; these are called master nodes (see below for full definition) and perform more tasks than regular nodes. Additionally, nodes are not tied to a specific network; nodes can switch to different blockchains practically at will, as is the case with multipool mining (see below).

Peer-to-Peer (P2P)/P2P Networks

A peer-to-peer network involves many computers working with each other to complete tasks. Peer-to-peer networks do not require a central authority and are an integral part of blockchain networks.

Private Key/Public Key

Cryptocurrency users will utilize two keys: a public key and a private key. Both keys are strings of letters and numbers. Once a user initiates their first transaction, a pair of public and private keys is created. The public key is used to receive cryptocurrencies, while the private key allows the user to carry out transactions from their account. Both keys are stored in a crypto wallet.

Protocol(s)

A protocol is a system or procedure that controls how something should be done. Within cryptocurrency, it is a governing layer of code. For example, a security protocol determines how security should be carried out, a blockchain protocol governs how blockchain acts and operates, and a Bitcoin protocol controls how Bitcoin functions.

Pump/Dump

A pump is a rapid upward price movement in a coin or token. A dump is a rapid downward price movement in a coin or token. "To the moon" refers to a massive pump or someone hoping for a massive pump.

Rank/Ranking

Cryptocurrencies are ranked by market cap; within the ranking system (you can think of it as a scoreboard), being in the top 10 is a kind of badge of honor. You'll often hear people say, "I think that coin can be in the top 10," and similar statements. Bitcoin has held the top spot pretty much indefinitely and likely will hold that top spot for the foreseeable future. Check out the coin rankings for yourself at any of the following sites or at any others you may know of:

- cryptoslate.com
- coingecko.com
- coinmarketcap.com

Satoshi Nakamoto

Satoshi Nakamoto is the individual, or possibly the group of individuals who created Bitcoin. Not much is known about this mysterious figure, and his anonymity has spawned countless conspiracy theories. While

Nakamoto lists himself as a 45-year-old male from Japan on an official peer-to-peer foundations website, he uses British idioms in his emails. Additionally, the timestamps of his work (fun fact: Nakamoto coded a secret message into the first mined block of Bitcoin) aligns better with someone based in the US or the UK. Most believe that his disappearance was planned (many have connected his work to biblical references), and others believe a governmental organization, such as the CIA, was linked to his disappearance. You should keep in mind that these are nothing more than fringe theories; however, what remains a fact is that the creator of Bitcoin currently holds a fortune worth more than $50 billion (Nakamoto owns 1.1 million Bitcoins), and if Bitcoin goes up another few hundred percent, this anonymous billionaire, the father of cryptocurrency, will be the richest person in the world.

Seed/Seed Phrase

A seed phrase is interchangeable with a mnemonic phrase (see below). Seed phrases are 12-to-24-word sequences that identify and represent a wallet. With it, you can never lose access to your account. If you forget it, there's no way to reset it or get it back. Anyone who has your seed phrase has full access to your wallet and cryptocurrency holdings.

Smart Contract(s)

Smart contracts are an essential part of the cryptocurrency world. A smart contract is a self-executing contract that is run on code. The terms of the contract and the execution are directly written into the smart contract by the code, and therefore this removes the issue of trust for all parties in the transaction. Transactions issued with smart contracts are irreversible and untraceable. These contracts can be used not just for managing cryptocurrency transactions but also for government voting systems, various other financial services, information storage, and many other industries.

Stablecoin

A stablecoin, similar to a pegged currency, is a coin or token that is designed to remain at the same price as a designated asset, typically a bank-issued currency. For example, USDT and DAI are two popular stablecoins that are pegged to the US dollar. So, 1 USDT is designed to always equal 1 US dollar. Stablecoins have very low volatility, typically earn a few percent interest (APY) per year and are generally a good place to store crypto holdings.

Technical Analysis

Technical analysis is a type of analysis that looks at technical indicators to predict price movement. Technical analysts use historical data from charts to make their predictions.

Ticker/Ticker Symbol

A ticker is a sequence of letters that identifies a specific coin or token. All stocks, as well as cryptocurrencies, have these ticker symbols. For example, Bitcoin is BTC and Ethereum is ETH.

Token(s)

A cryptocurrency token is a kind of digital currency that represents an asset, just like coins. However, while coins are built upon their own blockchain, tokens are built upon another blockchain. Many tokens use the Ethereum blockchain and are thus referred to as tokens, not coins. Coins are used only as money, while tokens can have a wider range of uses. Token uses are represented under subcategories, the most essential of which are security tokens, platform tokens, utility tokens, and governance tokens. Understanding tokens is an integral part of understanding what exactly you're trading, as well as understanding all uses of digital currencies, and for those reasons, we will take a look at the token types just mentioned.

- ◆ Security tokens represent legal ownership of an asset, whether digital or physical. The word "security" in security tokens doesn't mean security as in being safe, but rather, "security" refers to any financial instrument that holds value and can be traded. Basically, security tokens represent an investment or asset.

- ◆ Utility tokens are built into an existing protocol and can access the services of that protocol. Remember, protocols provide rules and a structure for nodes to follow, and utility tokens can be used for wider purposes than just as payment tokens. For example, utility tokens are commonly given to investors during an ICO. Then, later on, investors can use the utility tokens they received to pay on the platform they received the tokens from. The major thing to keep in mind is that utility tokens can do more than just serve as a means to buy or sell goods and services.

- ◆ Governance tokens are used to create and run a voting system for cryptocurrencies that allows system upgrades without a centralized owner.

- ◆ Payment (transactional) tokens are used solely to pay for goods and services.

Transaction

A transaction is any exchange between multiple parties. A cryptocurrency transaction involves one party buying a coin or token and another party selling that coin or token. Thousands of cryptocurrency transactions are completed per second.

Unpermissioned Ledger(s)

Unpermissioned ledgers are ledgers that have no single owner. The purpose of such a ledger is to allow for all the benefits of decentralization.

Wallet(s)

A wallet is the UI (the user interface, refer to definition) used to manage your account(s). For example, Coinbase and Exodus are common wallets.

Books

- Mastering Bitcoin – Andreas M. Antonopoulos

- The Internet of Money - Andreas M. Antonopoulos

- The Bitcoin Standard – Saifedean Ammous

- The Age of Cryptocurrency – Paul Vigna

- Digital Gold – Nathaniel Popper

- Bitcoin Billionaires – Ben Mezrich

- The Basics of Bitcoins and Blockchains – Antony Lewis

- Blockchain Revolution – Don Tapscott

- Cryptoassets - Chris Burniske and Jack Tatar

- The Age of Cryptocurrency - Paul Vigna

Exchanges

- Binance - binance.com (binance.us for US residents)

- Coinbase – coinbase.com

- Kraken – kraken.com

- Crypto – crypto.com

- Gemini – gemini.com

- eToro – etoro.com

Podcasts

- What Bitcoin Did by Peter McCormack (Bitcoin)

- Untold Stories (early stories)

- Unchained by Laura Shin (interviews)

- Baselayer by David Nage (discussions)

- The Breakdown by Nathaniel Whittemore (short)

- Crypto Campfire Podcast (relaxed)

- Ivan on Tech (updates)

- HASHR8 by Whit Gibbs (technical)

- Unqualified Opinions by Ryan Selkis (interviews)

News Services

- CoinDesk – coindesk.com

- CoinTelegraph – cointelegraph.com

- TodayOnChain – todayonchain.com

- NewsBTC – newsbtc.com

- Bitcoin Magazine – bitcoinmagazine.com

- Crypto Slate – cryptoslate.com

- Bitcoin.com – news.bitcoin.com

- Blockonomi – blockonomi.com

Charting Services

- TradingView – tradingview.com

- CryptoView – cryptoview.com

- Altrady – Altrady.com

- Coinigy – Coinigy.com

- Coin Trader - Cointrader.pro

- CryptoWatch – Cryptowat.ch

YouTube Channels

- Benjamin Cowen

  https://www.youtube.com/channel/UCRvqjQPSeaWn-uEx-w0XOIg

- Coin Bureau

  https://www.youtube.com/c/CoinBureau

- Forflies

  https://www.youtube.com/c/Forflies

- DataDash

  https://www.youtube.com/c/DataDash

- Sheldon Evans

  https://www.youtube.com/c/SheldonEvansx

¨ Anthony Pompliano

https://www.youtube.com/channel/UCevXpeL8cNyAnww-NqJ4m2w

¨ Aimstone

https://www.youtube.com/channel/UC7S9sRXUBrtF0nKTvLY3fwg/abou t

¨ Lark Davis

https://www.youtube.com/channel/UCl2oCaw8hdR_kbqyqd2klIA

¨ Altcoin Daily

https://www.youtube.com/channel/UCbLhGKVY-

bJPcawebgtNfbw

References

-, E. M., By, -, Edith M.Edith is an investment writer, M., E., & writer, E. is an investment. (2021, February 10). *Edith M.* Forex Academy. Retrieved September 29, 2021, from https://www.forex.academy/detailed-breakdown-of-bitcoins-four-years-cycles/.

Bajpai, P. (2021, September 8). *Countries where bitcoin is legal and illegal.* Investopedia. Retrieved September 29, 2021, from https://www.investopedia.com/articles/forex/041515/countries-where-bitcoin-legal-illegal.asp.

Banks consume over three times more energy than Bitcoin, according to researcher. Bitcoinist.com. (2018, August 23). Retrieved September 29, 2021, from https://bitcoinist.com/banks-consume-energy-bitcoin/.

Benson, J. (2020, November 24). *What makes the Bitcoin Blockchain secure?* Decrypt. Retrieved September 29, 2021, from https://decrypt.co/resources/what-makes-the-bitcoin-blockchain-secure.

Berlatsky, N. (2015). *Bitcoin.* Greenhaven Press, a part of Gale, Cengage Learning.

Best, R. de. (2021, September 14). *Blockchain wallets 2011-2021.* Statista. Retrieved September 29, 2021, from https://www.statista.com/statistics/647374/worldwide-blockchain-wallet-users/.

Binance Academy. (2020, November 16). *What makes a blockchain secure?* Binance Academy. Retrieved September 29, 2021, from https://academy.binance.com/en/articles/what-makes-a-blockchain-secure.

Binance Academy. (2021, August 18). *What is a blockchain consensus algorithm?* Binance Academy. Retrieved September 29, 2021, from https://academy.binance.com/en/articles/what-is-a-blockchain-consensus-algorithm.

Bink, A., & Wire, N. M. (2021, May 22). *What is Bitcoin and How does it use fossil fuels?* Eyewitness News (WEHT/WTVW). Retrieved September 29, 2021, from

https://www.tristatehomepage.com/news/national-world/what-is-bitcoin-and-how-does-it-use-fossil-fuels/#:

bitaddress.org. (n.d.). Retrieved September 29, 2021, from https://www.bitaddress.org/.

Bitcoin explained - Chapter 7: BITCOINS Scalability. Investerest. (n.d.). Retrieved September 29, 2021, from https://investerest.vontobel.com/en-dk/articles/13323/bitcoin-explained---chapter-7-bitcoins-scalability/.

Bitcoin verification latency - iang.org. (n.d.). Retrieved September 29, 2021, from https://www.iang.org/papers/BitcoinLatency.pdf.

Bitcoin.comBitcoin.com is author of this content, Bitcoin.com, & Bitcoin.com is author of this content. (2018, November 29). *The US government is powerless to block bitcoin addresses - the Bitcoin news.* The Bitcoin News - Bitcoin and Blockchain News. Retrieved September 29, 2021, from https://thebitcoinnews.com/the-us-government-is-powerless-to-block-bitcoin-addresses/.

Bitcoin: A Peer-to-Peer electronic cash system. (n.d.). Retrieved September 29, 2021, from https://bitcoin.org/bitcoin.pdf.

Bitcoin: A Peer-to-Peer electronic cash system. (n.d.). Retrieved September 29, 2021, from https://bitcoin.org/bitcoin.pdf.

Blockchain use cases IN 2021: Real world industry applications. ConsenSys. (n.d.). Retrieved September 29, 2021, from https://consensys.net/blockchain-use-cases/.

Blockchain use Cases: IBM BLOCKCHAIN. Blockchain use cases | IBM Blockchain. (2021, July 6). Retrieved September 29, 2021, from https://www.ibm.com/blockchain/use-cases/.

Bloomenthal, A. (2021, September 29). *What determines the price of 1 bitcoin?* Investopedia. Retrieved September 29, 2021, from https://www.investopedia.com/tech/what-determines-value-1-bitcoin/.

Buntinx, J. P. (2016, December 20). *Top 4 cryptocurrency projects created before bitcoin*. The Merkle News. Retrieved September 29, 2021, from https://themerkle.com/top-4-cryptocurrency-projects-created-ahead-of-bitcoin/.

Carmen, J. D. (2021, September 27). *Bitcoin and Altcoin market cycles*. The Hub on ACCOINTING.com. Retrieved September 29, 2021, from https://www.accointing.com/the-hub/market-analysis/2021/bitcoin-and-altcoin-market-cycles/.

Carmen, J. D. (2021, September 27). *Bitcoin and Altcoin market cycles*. The Hub on ACCOINTING.com. Retrieved September 29, 2021, from https://www.accointing.com/the-hub/market-analysis/2021/bitcoin-and-altcoin-market-cycles/.

Caselin, B. (2021, June 7). *Are altcoins a distraction or is bitcoin just outdated?* LinkedIn. Retrieved September 29, 2021, from https://www.linkedin.com/pulse/altcoins-distraction-bitcoin-just-outdated-ben-caselin/.

Castillo, M. del. (2020, February 27). *Blockchain 50*. Forbes. Retrieved September 29, 2021, from https://www.forbes.com/sites/michaeldelcastillo/2020/02/19/blockchain-50/?sh=355d30b7553d.

Chishti, S., O'Hanlon, S., Bradley, B., Jockle, J., & Patrick, D. (2020). *FinTech for Dummies*. Wiley.

Cobb, C. (2004). *Cryptography for dummies*. John Wiley & Sons.

Daniel Phillips, S. C. (2021, September 14). *Can a country actually ban bitcoin?* Decrypt. Retrieved September 29, 2021, from https://decrypt.co/37366/can-a-country-actually-ban-bitcoin.

A detailed breakdown of Bitcoin's four year cycles. Hacker Noon. (n.d.). Retrieved September 29, 2021, from https://hackernoon.com/a-detailed-breakdown-of-bitcoins-four-year-cycles-icp3z0q.

Digital currency Business E-gold indicted for money laundering and illegal money transmitting. (n.d.). Retrieved September 29, 2021, from https://www.justice.gov/archive/criminal/cybercrime/press-releases/2007/egoldIndict.htm.

Edwards, J. (2021, September 21). *Bitcoin's price history*. Investopedia. Retrieved September 29, 2021, from https://www.investopedia.com/articles/forex/121815/bitcoins-price-history.asp.

Edwood, F. (2020, October 23). *Why low latency is important for cryptocurrency exchanges, explained*. Cointelegraph. Retrieved September 29, 2021, from https://cointelegraph.com/explained/why-low-latency-is-important-for-cryptocurrency-exchanges-explained.

Factors affecting cryptocurrency mining profit. EastShore Mining Devices. (2020, May 6). Retrieved September 29, 2021, from https://www.eastshore.xyz/factors-affecting-cryptocurrency-mining-profit/.

Fiat vs. crypto & digital currencies. Gemini. (n.d.). Retrieved September 29, 2021, from https://www.gemini.com/cryptopedia/fiat-vs-crypto-digital-currencies.

Five reasons why governments won't ban Bitcoin and can't STOP CRYPTO. Coin24h.com. (2020, November 12). Retrieved September 29, 2021, from https://www.coin24h.com/bitcoin/five-reasons-why-governments-wont-ban-bitcoin-and-cant-stop-crypto/.

Global Bitcoin nodes distribution. Bitnodes. (n.d.). Retrieved September 29, 2021, from https://bitnodes.io/.

Griffith, K. (2014, April 17). *A quick history of cryptocurrencies bbtc - before bitcoin*. Bitcoin Magazine: Bitcoin News, Articles, Charts, and Guides. Retrieved September 29, 2021, from https://bitcoinmagazine.com/business/quick-history-cryptocurrencies-bbtc-bitcoin-1397682630.

Gupta, S. (2021, March 23). *Why is hashing your top priority for data security?* Audienceplay. Retrieved September 29, 2021, from https://www.audienceplay.com/blog/hashing/.

How many bitcoin users are there? How Many People Use & Own Bitcoins? (2021). (n.d.). Retrieved September 29, 2021, from https://www.buybitcoinworldwide.com/how-many-bitcoin-users/.

How much energy does bitcoin actually consume? Harvard Business Review. (2021, May 6). Retrieved September 29, 2021, from https://hbr.org/2021/05/how-much-energy-does-bitcoin-actually-consume.

How to create a Bitcoin paper wallet. dummies. (2021, July 6). Retrieved September 29, 2021, from https://www.dummies.com/personal-finance/create-bitcoin-paper-wallet/.

IntoTheBlock. (n.d.). Retrieved September 29, 2021, from https://app.intotheblock.com/coin/BTC/deep-dive?group=network&chart=transactions.

Jordan Tuwiner Last updated September 10, 2021. (n.d.). *Who accepts bitcoin? 11 major companies.* 9 Major Companies Who Accept Bitcoin (Spend Bitcoin 2021). Retrieved September 29, 2021, from https://www.buybitcoinworldwide.com/who-accepts-bitcoin/.

Laurence, T. (2019). *Blockchain.* For Dummies, a Wiley brand.

Maritz, P. (2020, June 6). *Learn how to calculate your crypto mining profitability.* Cointelligence. Retrieved September 29, 2021, from https://www.cointelligence.com/content/crypto-mining-profitability/.

Permissioned vs Permissionless Blockchains. 101 Blockchains. (2021, August 15). Retrieved September 29, 2021, from https://101blockchains.com/permissioned-vs-permissionless-blockchains/.

Quast, J. (2021, May 21). *Crypto crash 2021: 2 lessons from Bitcoin's history.* The Motley Fool. Retrieved September 29, 2021, from https://www.fool.com/investing/2021/05/21/crypto-crash-2021-3-lessons-from-bitcoin-history/.

Regan, N. L. & J. (2021, June 18). How safe is bitcoin, really? Retrieved September 29, 2021, from https://www.avg.com/en/signal/is-bitcoin-safe.

Reporter, S. (2020, December 17). *How much money is in the world?* The Sun. Retrieved September 29, 2021, from https://www.thesun.co.uk/money/13497643/how-much-money-in-the-.

Rhodes, D. (2021, March 21). *What is margin trading? A complete guide for beginners.* Komodo Academy | En. Retrieved September 29, 2021, from https://komodoplatform.com/en/academy/margin-trading/.

SoFi. (2021, May 18). *Bitcoin hash rate and why it matters.* SoFi. Retrieved September 29, 2021, from https://www.sofi.com/learn/content/bitcoin-hash-rate/.

Spegele, B., & Ostroff, C. (2021, May 21). *Bitcoin miners are giving new life to OLD fossil-fuel power plants.* The Wall Street Journal. Retrieved September 29, 2021, from https://www.wsj.com/articles/bitcoin-miners-are-giving-new-life-to-old-fossil-fuel-power-plants-11621594803.

Wallis, J., & BitcoinWolf. (2021, June 20). *Real world blockchain use cases - 46 blockchain applications.* 101 Blockchains. Retrieved September 29, 2021, from https://101blockchains.com/blockchain-applications/.

Yahoo! (n.d.). *Cryptocurrency has 'NO intrinsic value' and investors could 'lose all your MONEY', SAYS Bank of england chief.* Yahoo! Finance. Retrieved September 29, 2021, from https://finance.yahoo.com/news/cryptocurrency-no-intrinsic-value-investors-163626143.html.

'Cryptourism, T. to D., & Uni. (2020, September 19). *Analyst: 1,500 bitcoins lost every day, less than 14 million coins will Ever circulate – News Bitcoin news.* Bitcoin News. Retrieved September 29, 2021, from https://news.bitcoin.com/analyst-1500-bitcoins-lost-every-day-less-than-14-million-coins-will-ever-circulate.

Endnotes

i i Matthäus Wander, CC BY-SA 3.0 <https://creativecommons.org/licenses/by-sa/3.0>, via Wikimedia Commons

ii C. (2020, February 2). *Friction* [Illustration].

https://commons.wikimedia.org/wiki/File:Friction.png

iii "How Many Bitcoins Are There?" *How Many Bitcoins Are There? How Many Left to Mine? (2021)*, www.buybitcoinworldwide.com/how-many-bitcoins-are-there/.

"Bitnodes: Global Bitcoin Nodes Distribution." https://bitnodes.io/. Accessed 30 Aug. 2021.

v "You would need $21 million to attack Bitcoin for a day - Decrypt." 31 Jan. 2020, https://decrypt.co/18012/you-would-need-21-million-to-attack-bitcoin-for-a-day. Accessed 30 Aug

vi Renepick, CC BY-SA 4.0 <https://creativecommons.org/licenses/by-sa/4.0>, via Wikimedia Commons

vii Original image; based on the following imageassets:

Mauro Bieg / GNU GPL / File:Server-based-network.svg

Ludovic Ferre / PDM / File:P2P-network.svg

Michel Banki / CC BY-SA 4.0 / File:Client-server_Vs_peer-to-peer_-_ en.png

viii Ladislav Mecir at English Wikipedia, CC BY-SA 3.0 <https://creativecommons.org/licenses/by-sa/3.0>, via Wikimedia Commons

ix *Bitcoin.com*, news.bitcoin.com/despite-bitcoins-price-drop-high-powered-mining-rigs-still-profit/.

x x Nickboariu, CC BY-SA 4.0 <https://creativecommons.org/licenses/by-sa/4.0>, via Wikimedia Commons

xi "Bitcoin Mining Distribution 3 | Download Scientific Diagram." https://www.researchgate.net/figure/Bitcoin-Mining-Distribution-3_fig3_328150068. Accessed 2 Sep. 2021.

xii https://www.morningbrew.com/emerging-tech/stories/2021/05/19/proofofstake-make-ethereum-9995-energyefficient-work

xiii "Best Staking CRYPTO [2021]: POPULAR Staking Coins and How to Find Them!" *CoinMarketExpert*, 28 June 2021, coinmarketexpert.com/best-staking-crypto/.

xiv https://www.forexkarma.com/forex-leverage.html

xv Jonlaw16, CC BY-SA 4.0 <https://creativecommons.org/licenses/by-sa/4.0>, via Wikimedia Commons

xvi Bucque, Patrick t, et al. "How Many Active Crypto Traders Are There across the Globe?" *CH&Co*, Www.chappuishalder.com.

cCredit: unfolded.io, data from tradingview.com

xviii https://www.telegraph.co.uk/technology/2021/01/22/weird-world-bitcoin-whales-2500-people-control-40pc-market/.

[xix] Realtrafficsource, R., Toochukwu, scam, A. iT. gift card, Auget, Prothro, B., Nicolas, Anthony, Petty, D., Albert, M., Rosenberg, M., Bitcoin, B. C. with, Yair, ClearMax, Hutt, T., Ferreira, M., Christian, D., Bee, Smith, J., Tatyana, ... Kathleen. (2020, October 19). *250+ places that accept bitcoin PAYMENT (Online & PHYSICAL Companies)*. ICOholder Blog. Retrieved September 29, 2021, from https://icoholder.com/blog/places-accept-bitcoin/.

[xx] Kurzycz http://www.kurzy.cz/, CC BY-SA 4.0

<https://creativecommons.org/licenses/by-sa/4.0>, via Wikimedia Commons

[xxi] Image creators cannot be identified; the base concept has been replicated in many different formats.

[xxii] Matthäus Wander, CC BY-SA 3.0 <https://creativecommons.org/licenses/by-sa/3.0>, via Wikimedia Commons

[xxiii] "Top 100 Richest Bitcoin Addresses and Bitcoin Distribution." *BitInfoCharts*, 25 Sept. 2021, bitinfocharts.com/top-100-richest-bitcoin-addresses.html.

[xxiv] "File:Bitcoin-Cash-Logo-Horizontal.svg." *Wikimedia Commons*, commons.wikimedia.org/wiki/File:Bitcoin-cash-logo-horizontal.svg.

[xxv] "United States Demographic Statistics ...."

https://www.infoplease.com/us/census/demographic-statistics.

[xxv] "• Chart: How Many Consumers Own Cryptocurrency? | Statista." 20 Aug. 2018, https://www.statista.com/chart/15137/how-many-consumers-own-cryptocurrency/.

[xxv] "Blockchain.com." https://www.blockchain.com/. Accessed 9 Jun. 2021.

Per aspera ad astra.

Lightning Source UK Ltd.
Milton Keynes UK
UKHW020634241122
412716UK00006B/175/J

9 780578 306049